LANDSCAPE MANAGEMENT AND MAINTENANCE

Landscape Management and Maintenance

A Guide to its Costing and Organization

John Parker
and
Peter Bryan

Gower Technical

© John Parker and Peter Bryan 1989

Published by
Gower Technical
Gower Publishing Company Limited
Gower House
Croft Road
Aldershot
Hants GU11 3HR
England

Gower Publishing Company
Old Post Road
Brookfield
Vermont 05036
USA

British Library Cataloguing-in-Publication Data
Parker, John, *1936–*
    Landscape management and maintenance.
    1. Landscape design. Manuals
    I. Title II. Bryan, Peter, *1946–*
    712

ISBN 0 566 09018 X

Printed in Great Britain by Billing & Sons Limited, Worcester

CONTENTS

systems – quality control – Appendix I: Application for
inclusion on approved list of contractors.

INTRODUCTION

Doing anything in public, from acting on the stage to mending the road, takes a certain amount of courage. Gardening in public is no exception and has the added risk that the English are a nation of self-professed gardening experts. Thus municipal gardeners have to do their work in the public gaze and whatever they actually do, there is bound to be someone looking on who thinks he or she knows better. After several years of serving the public we have grown to accept this as a fact of life, a fact which we even enjoy – most of the time at least! However, relatively few people have an understanding, or even an interest, in the art or science of managing public parks or open spaces as attractive areas of landscape that are growing, developing and constantly changing.

This book is not about how to tend the trees and shrubs or how to cut the grass, although it will mention these by way of illustration. It is not a guide to horticultural excellence, but it does try to set horticultural principles into an economic framework. It will, we hope, help the reader to put a cost against various levels and methods of landscape husbandry and tackle the questions of what labour and equipment is needed and how they should be organized and managed.

Finally, it examines how the manager must always have a broader view and be looking ahead at how landscapes will be changing and what our needs and uses of open spaces will be in the future. Social habits are constantly changing and population movements also mean that the use of almost any park or open space is in a constant state of flux. Detecting the moves and responding to them is just as much part of the art of the landscape manager as the husbandry of the landscape itself, but is perhaps the more important if our green spaces are to play their full part in the quality of English national life.

Chapter 1

LANDSCAPE MAINTENANCE AND MANAGEMENT

The Process of Management

In almost any area of human endeavour, the process of management can be distilled down to:

setting the objectives
planning the operation
putting it into action
monitoring the action and replanning as necessary.

In landscape, the process of putting the plan into action, the work of the day-to-day maintenance, is the part that takes the most time and energy as well as cost. It is also the part that is the most obvious sign of any management at all and so it is not surprising that it tends to dominate our attention, sometimes to the extent that the overall objective, the whole purpose of the exercise, can become obscured or even forgotten.

The efficiency of the day-to-day maintenance is obviously important in terms of cost, but this can be to little real effect if it produces the wrong or undesirable results. Setting the objectives is therefore an essential first step if the manager is going to steer the ship of maintenance in the right course.

1

Setting the Objectives

The aims of landscape are many and varied, and gardens and open space seldom serve a single purpose. Thus any area of amenity land may be managed to provide:

pleasant views or appearance
screening or shelter
nature conservation
horticultural excellence
botanical variety and education
space for sport or recreation
job-creation or leisure gardening

Many of these purposes will be immediately self-evident from the layout or use of the land but, in many others, the circumstances may have changed since the site was first laid out and so obscured the original purpose. Therefore, whenever the maintenance is being planned or reviewed, it is essential to have a clear idea of the use and functions of the land.

The private landowner will probably have no particular difficulty in deciding what he or she wishes to achieve but, even so, writing down the objectives as a form of maintenance brief will often help to highlight the essentials of the routine work. For public open space the process is rather more complicated. Different individuals or groups will have different ideas and aspirations for the land and these have to be offset against the limitations of funds and even the political aspirations of the local authority – some may favour nature conservation and others seek relative formality or horticultural perfection.

With the potential for a wide range of views, the landscape manager may be tempted merely to fall back on his personal preferences or simply persist with the past and established regimes. However, it is important to try to assess clients' wishes, even if they are difficult to determine, and so have a firmer base on which to allocate or seek resources. This can be done in a number of ways including:

surveys of the numbers using a park and the ways in which they use it
questionnaires or opinion surveys

meetings with community groups or leaders.

These methods of canvassing users' opinions all tend to suffer from the disadvantage that the public at large is strongly influenced by what already exists and is unable to envisage any alternative. To some extent this difficulty can be overcome by carefully designing the questionnaire, but there is also advantage in developing experimental areas as public demonstrations.

Although a well-designed survey can give a good indication of public preferences, these preferences may not be those of the client who will have to make the final decision. In the case of most public open space this will normally be an elected council or committee who, while they represent the public, are under a wide range of different pressures for the allocation of resources. One of these pressures may be the professional landscape manager, so there may be a triangle of forces and influences as shown below.

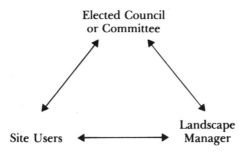

In practice this diagram is a simplification and there are likely to be a number of other interconnecting strands of influence involving local user groups, political associations, trade unions and the many others on the stage of democratic life. These influences can be very frustrating to the landscape manager particularly if he is too committed to imposing his own aspirations onto the landscape. However, the true landscape manager must learn to work just as much, if not more, with people as with plants, and recognize the vital role of educating people's perceptions of landscape as well as just managing it. This process of education has many facets but the manager

Table 1.1   *Approximate annual labour inputs for landscape types*

	Man-days per year/hectare
Amenity woodland	0 – 5
Extensive parkland	10 – 20
Sports and recreation grounds	30 – 50
Flowering shrubs	100 – 200
Annual bedding	1000 +

should try to present the options as clearly as possible so that the decision-makers can make their judgements on the basis of the best available information. Costs are likely to be foremost in many people's minds and means of considering value for money are suggested later in this chapter.

Costs and Style of Maintenance

The style and intensity of maintenance will sometimes have a much greater effect on the cost of upkeep than the organization or efficiency of carrying it out. In general terms, the more natural or informal the layout and maintenance, the lower the cost. Conversely the more formal, or removed from nature, the more expensive will be the result. For instance, from the figures shown in Table 1.1 the choice of summer bedding instead of flowering shrubs could increase the costs more than threefold.

The detail or complexity of a site's layout will also influence its maintenance cost, quite apart from the type of landscape and its degree of formality. Simple layouts are much more easily maintained by powerful machinery with considerably less labour requirements for a given area. More complex layouts, with relatively small spaces, require a much greater use of small equipment and manual labour and are consequently much more expensive to maintain. For example, broad open sweeps of gang-mown grass will require approximately 10–20 man-hours/year/hectare, but if the area is divided up into small parts, perhaps including numerous obstructions, and has to be mown with a 'ride-on' triple mower, the man-hours per year will be doubled at least.

While they are easier to maintain, the broad simple layouts of gang-mown grass are generally less interesting and attractive and, in particular, have been criticized for providing little in the way of nature conservation. They have aptly been described as 'green deserts' and different mowing techniques have been adopted to provide variation in the sward and encourage the establishment of wildflowers. These techniques, which can vary from hay sward management to suspending routine mowing at certain times of the year, have the potential to save time on overall maintenance. However, when compared with the simplicity of regular mowing, they tend to complicate the operations with additional and special machines having to be brought in. As a result the apparent potential for savings are not always achieved and the advantages are a more interesting variation in the swards, seasonal as well as biological, rather than any significant cost saving in terms of total labour inputs (see Table 1.2).

Some economic advantage may arise through the redistribution of the workload throughout the year, particularly if the mowing regime reduces the volume of mowing at the peak of the season. Thus in the example in Table 1.2, the peak summer workload for gang-mowing is reduced by approximately 14 per cent in the second alternative, even though the total work-hours are only slightly reduced.

Much more significant savings could be achieved simply by reducing the total number of cuts, but this would alter the overall character of the site and perhaps not make it suitable for the original use. More 'natural' approaches of grazing or hay cropping can also be very cost-effective, and indeed may be more appropriate in rural or informal situations. Unfortunately, the practical difficulties can be significant and include:

- modern agricultural sward management, for high productivity, will not usually provide the diverse swards that are sought for amenity 'meadows'
- livestock in public areas can frighten the public (e.g. young bullocks); or can be worried by them and, particularly, dogs
- the costs of providing fencing and water can be considerable
- litter and other rubbish in a hay crop can harm cattle and damage machinery.

For these reasons 'agricultural' maintenance is sometimes quite

Table 1.2 *Simple mowing or variation?*

	Machine and labour hours per year
Alternative A. The 'green desert'	
1 hectare of clear gangmowing	
Mowing 20 cuts @ ·4 hours	8
Travel and set up 20 @ ·3 hours	6
Total	14 hrs/yr
Alternative B. Gangmowing and hay meadow	
·75 hectare of clear gangmowing	
Mowing 20 cuts @ ·3 hours	6
Travel and set up 20 @ ·3 hours	6
sub-total	12
·25 hectare of meadow culture	
Mowing 3 cuts with tractor mounted flail @ ·3 hours	·9
Travel and set up 3 @ ·3 hours	·9
sub-total	1.8
Total	13.8 hrs/yr

Note:
Extra cost may be involved in raking off grass cuttings in the hay meadow.

difficult to arrange and is often only practised as a means of bringing livestock into country parks and the like for the interest of visitors.

Value for Money

Value for money is something that we frequently search for but is very difficult to define in precise terms. More often than not it depends a great deal on personal tastes or attitudes so that universal approval is rare. For instance, relatively few of us can afford or wish to pay the premium for a first-class rail ticket and therefore it could be assumed that, for most of us, the ordinary fare gives the best return for the money. Some, however, have different views and are able to convince themselves – if they need convincing – that the extra comforts for the extra fare are indeed value for money.

In landscape maintenance there is a similar range of attitudes so that making the best value-judgement is a very subjective exercise. Often in the absence of any established framework for this subjectivity, it is easier merely to base the decisions on cost and assume that low cost is the only desirable objective.

This particular attitude is all the more easily sustained because the costs are relatively simple to define, but the outputs or benefits are often nearly impossible to put in such precise terms. Thus it is easy to establish the cost of planting and subsequently maintaining a well-designed strip of roadside verge but it is very difficult indeed to put a value on the pleasure it might give to road users or people living in the vicinity (see Figure 1.1).

Various attempts have been made to assess the value of landscape by indirect means, such as the value of houses in a tree-lined avenue compared with those where there are no trees. The number of people visiting different parks could give an indication of how much it is valued, and surveys of how far people are prepared to travel to reach a park or piece of countryside have been used as well. Unfortunately all these methods take a good deal of time and can be unsatisfactory because of other more dominant factors (e.g. the tree-lined avenue may be nearer to shops or schools).

Much more frequently the choice concerns how to care for an established landscape and a practical approach for day-to-day use is to list and compare the benefits, or otherwise, of different levels of maintenance. The starting point for this would normally be the existing levels of upkeep and this, in turn, is likely to be heavily influenced by the layout of the site and the type and intensity of use. As an example, the lawns in a formal quadrangle of a school or college might presently be mown and boxed off at least once a week. This would give an annual cost in man-hours of:

24 mowings @ 2 hours = 48 hours

Alternatives of around ± 20 per cent might have the following effects:

Planting a road verge with standard trees.

Plain verge   ⇄   Planted avenue
                    or

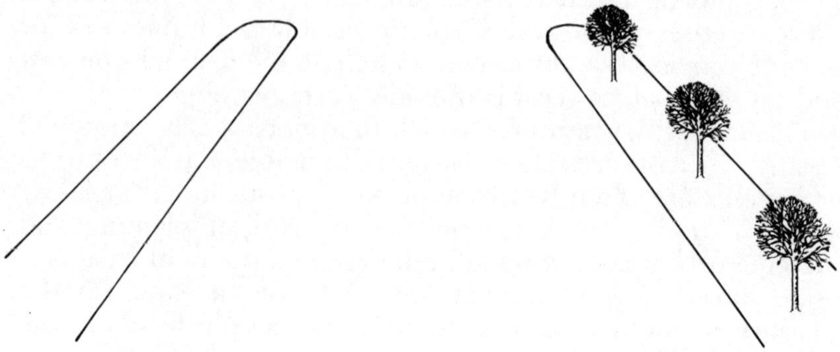

Extra costs (say, over 20 years)	*Benefits*	
Supply, planting and caring for the trees.	Visual	more pleasant scene, screening of houses, variation in shade.
Trimming or spraying the base.		
(Mowing round the obstacles compensated by less grass growth).	Physical	CO_2 and dust extraction, shelter, shade, etc.
Total probably equivalent to the cost of 4 to 5 man hours per tree.	Others	Wildlife habitat, educational value, sense of place etc.
Extra costs might arise from leaf fall problems, damage to paving, drains and underground services.		

For a 100-metre stretch of verge (trees spaced at 5-metre intervals) the annual cost would be equivalent to:

$$\frac{4 \text{ to } 5 \times 20}{20 \text{ years}} = 4 \text{ or } 5 \text{ man-hours per year}$$

Subsequent costs unlikely to fall because of the need for safety inspections, possible pruning or even felling and replacing.

Figure 1.1   *Value for money?*

29 mowings @ 2 hours = 58 hours
'smarter', more formal lawn
'stripes' obvious for more of the time

or: 19 mowings @ 2 hours = 38 hours

longer grass but still with an even finish
'stripes' less obvious between mowings

Many people would probably feel that the lower mowing frequency was adequate and most visitors might not notice the difference without their attention being drawn to it. Thus if the 'saved' hours could truly be saved and used profitably elsewhere, the 19 cuts per year would be better value for money than the other alternatives. Reducing the inputs still further might give:

14 mowings @ 2.3* hours = 30.8 hours
slightly longer grass
heavier layer of cuttings after each mowing

or: 8 mowings @ 2.4* hours = 19.2 hours

longer grass between mowings
. need to use a rotary of flail mower to cope with the growth
grass cuttings a distinct problem, blocking drains, etc.

*increased mowing time to account for extra vegetation.

Thus, although the lower mowing frequency might save 20 per cent or so on the cost, the 'product' would be much less acceptable, or not fit for the purpose, and therefore unlikely to be value for money.

This same approach to maintenance standards can be applied to other features like hedges and shrub borders. Applying less or more attention to a hedge will tend to give it a slightly neater, or more ragged, or natural appearance, and judgements can be made on how important this is in any given situation.

On shrub borders the cost variations will tend to centre on the amount of time that is spent on weed control or clearing accumulated rubbish or (non-biological) litter. Perfection can be extremely expensive and something falling short of ideal is more likely to be a sensible compromise. For instance, the weed and litter may be able to be kept at acceptable levels by spending an hour once in four weeks in clearing it up. To reduce the weed and litter presence significantly would almost certainly need attention once every two weeks and the job would still take almost as long, i.e. the cost would be doubled for relatively little advantage. Even worse, to keep the border completely litter-free might need twice weekly or even daily attention with costs increased ten-fold or more.

In some situations (near open air markets, next to school tuckshops, etc.) these levels of attention are essential to achieve a reasonable standard, but the open space manager will obviously look to other means of trying to discourage the littering or altering the planting and layout so that it is less of a problem.

Value for Money on Playing Fields and Sports Grounds

In maintaining sports fields and playing surfaces for outdoor sport it is relatively easy to ascertain the costs to the users and therefore have a firmer base on which to judge value for money. However, for those sports that require very precise and accurate playing surfaces, the choice in levels of upkeep is somewhat restricted. For sports such as:

Bowls
Lawn tennis
Golf and putting
Cricket
Hockey

the maintenance must be at an adequate minimum to provide a smooth and even surface. There is, of course, a difference in standard between Wimbledon Centre Court and the local tennis club but both must be weed-free, smooth and firm if there is to be any chance of playing a reasonable game of tennis. In addition, the Wimbledon courts must retain these qualities, as close as possible to perfection, but also sustain the tremendous wear of many first-class matches in a short period of time.

Even at club level the cost of maintaining a grass tennis court is likely to be equivalent to around 100 man-hours of skilled work a year. As both these costs, and more particularly the skills, are relatively hard to come by, many clubs and players are now turning to synthetic surfaces. Although the capital costs are high (apart from wicket strips) and are not likely to be recouped in terms of maintenance saving (see Table 1.3 below), they are much more effective in providing a safe and reliable surface, if necessary throughout the whole year. (See later section for further discussion on the economics of synthetic surfaces.)

The Effect of Intensity of Use of Grass Pitches

Even for the less demanding sports there is a basic need to provide a minimum level of playing surface for satisfactory use. Therefore, the costs of maintenance are relatively high even if the pitch is only lightly used and the costs do not increase *pro rata* according to the level of use. The impact of the relatively high costs of initial provision (the standing charges) are even more marked if the capital cost of the land is taken into account but, on the basis of the maintenance alone, unit costs are lower if the pitch is relatively well used. This is shown in Table 1.4.

On the basis of this cost pattern it is sensible to make as much use as possible of any pitch and not, for instance, reserve it for one special match a week. In practice, however, there are social and biological/physical limits on the amount of use that can be made. Most sport is a social activity and team games in particular are normally played at specific 'social' times when the

Table 1.3 *Capital costs of synthetic surfaces compared with maintenance costs of a grass equivalent*

	Capital cost	Grass maintenance cost	Potential 'pay back' period
Cricket wicket	£2–3000	£1000	2–3 years
Tennis court	£10–20,000	£1000	10–20 years
Bowling green	£30–50,000	£2000	15–25 years
Hockey pitch	£150–300,000	£1500	over 100 years

Approximate 1987 prices.

Table 1.4 *Maintenance costs of a football pitch
under light and heavy use*

(say 1 hectare)	3 hours use per week	8 hours use per week
Gang-mowing	£160	£160
Fertiliser and weed killing	£10	£40
Setting out and remarking	£120	£170
Winter care of worn areas, spiking, etc.	£50	£300
Spring renovation (seeding or returfing, etc.)	£30	£60
Total cost per year	£370	£730
Hours use (assuming a 25 week season)	75	200
Cost per hours use	£4.9	£3.6

Based on 1988 costs

players are free from their work or family commitments. Thus there is likely to be a strong demand to play matches, of football, hockey or rugby, on Saturday afternoon or Sunday morning, and relatively little demand at other times of the week.

School Playing Fields and Dual Use

School playing fields are something of an exception in this respect as their use can be spread over a longer period of the week, although there is still a preference towards afternoons or certain days of the week. The fact that school playing fields tend to be used less, or not at all, at weekends, in the evenings or school holidays, makes them apparently ideal for dual-use proposals, i.e. for letting to adult or non-school teams outside school hours. Provided there are no physical constraints on the level of use (see below), this can often be a good arrangement for the benefit of both the school and the clubs. For instance:

• costs of upkeep and provision can be spread over larger base
• additional income from lettings can be used to provide better playing surfaces

- linking of school and club sports encourages young people to continue with the sport when they leave school
- the presence of other people on site, outside school hours, tends to discourage trespass and vandalism.

There are of course some problems:

- pitch sizes, particularly on primary schools, are not suitable for club use
- changing and social facilities (bar or clubroom) are not usually particularly suitable, or even available, for adult use
- special arrangements have to be made to unlock part of the school building or provide hot water for showers
- the sense of ownership and allegiance to the site is reduced for both parties and provision for spectators are usually inadequate, particularly for car parking.

Where there is a will these difficulties can usually be overcome but they can be made much easier if the layout of the pitches and the changing facilities have been designed with dual use in mind. For example:

- the changingrooms can be built as a separate part of the school building with independent or easily isolated heating and water systems
- a separate clubroom/pavilion with changing facilities can be built under licence by the sports club on a separate part of the site
- all the sports facilities, indoors and outdoors, can be provided next door or close to the school but separately managed as a sports centre for general use but with priority allocation to the school during school hours.

Biological/Physical Limitations on Playing Field Use

Even if the social constraints on use can be overcome there are still biological and physical limits on the use that grass pitches can bear without becoming damaged beyond repair. The actual limits can be stretched to some extent by good and skilful groundsmanship (and firm control over use in wet or frosty weather) but the strongest limiting factor is the nature of the underlying soil and its drainage.

The regulations of the Department of Education and Science for the provision of school playing fields assume seven hours' use a week during school term and this is probably a reasonable average figure. However, many badly drained pitches may not be able to average more than one hour's use a week through the winter months and even be completely unplayable for two or three months in bad weather. Conversely, well-drained and constructed pitches can sustain as much as 20 hours' use a week.

It is not the purpose of this book to describe the various construction and drainage methods to achieve good wearing ability. However, the costs of these measures have two main benefits:

1   increasing the chances of the pitches being suitable for use at a particular time (see Appendix I on the cost-benefit of underground drainage)
2   increasing the total use capacity of the pitch.

These two advantages usually come together but have a different importance according to the circumstances. For instance, a professional football club may not be particularly interested in increasing the total use capacity of their pitch but be extremely anxious that the pitch should be fit for use at the time of their fixtures. On the other hand, for a school or community pitch, it is more important that the surface can sustain long and regular use.

Synthetic Surfaces

If sustained use is of paramount importance, the only practical way of breaking through the 20 hours a week limit is to lay a synthetic surface. In the past these surfaces were extremely expensive, but recently a number of new materials have been developed. These are much cheaper to install and have playing characteristics that are closer to those of good quality turf and so make good alternatives to grass pitches for hockey and football. In theory they are capable of being used 24 hours a day for seven days a week but, for social reasons, the actual use is likely to be a good deal less. Even where floodlights are installed, and this is usually essential for full use, the average use is only likely to reach 6 or 7 hours a day, or 50 hours a week. Even this will require good management and tight programming and, in particular, generous provision of changing facilities to cope with a steady stream of players at peak times.

Revenue and Capital Costs of Synthetic Surfaces

Contrary to popular opinion the synthetic pitches are not maintenance-free and, while they do not need the mowing and other work of grass pitches, they do need regular cleaning and minor repair to keep them in good order. These costs are lower than for a single grass pitch but are relatively minor in relation to the capital costs which dominate the economics of synthetic pitch provision. Actual costs of construction, and achievable use, will obviously vary according to the details of the construction and the type of surface. However, averages, in 1988 prices, are approximately:

	Capital cost	Potential hour's use per week	Capital cost per hour's use per week
Natural grass pitch with limited artificial drainage	£15,000	7	£2143
Natural grass pitch with sand carpet construction	£50,000	15	£3333
Synthetic grass pitch (with floodlighting)	£250,000	50	£5000

On this basis, the simple grass pitch appears to give better value for money but this does not take account of the capital value of the land and the large area that is needed to provide the equivalent use of a synthetic pitch in natural turf. In very round figures the sophisticated sand carpet, but natural pitch, will be equivalent to at least two simple grass pitches and a synthetic pitch will be equal to seven grass pitches. Therefore, if the land and construction costs are taken into account the total capital costs of providing the equivalent of seven grass pitches would be as in Table 1.5.

Table 1.5　*Comparative costs (land and construction) of the equivalent of seven grass pitches*

a.　7 natural grass pitches	7　×　(£15,000 + v)	or £105,000 + 7v
b.　3.5 sand carpet pitches	3·5 ×　(£50,000 + v)	or £175,000 + 3·5v
c.　1 synthetic pitch	1　×　(£250,000 + v)	or £250,000 + v

Where v = the value of the land per pitch.

Expressing these relationships in graphical form (see Figure 1.2) it is easy to see that grass pitches are only more economical when land prices are very low and, as land prices rise to even quite modest levels, synthetic pitches give a saving in total capital costs.

In practice, the land prices are likely to be up to £10,000 or so a pitch on agricultural or rural land but at least £100,000 in urban or town centres. This means that, on capital cost considerations alone, it is only likely to be economic to provide new grass pitches on agricultural-priced land.

For other reasons it is sensible to build playing fields on undeveloped or non-urban land. Playing fields are a good land use on the urban/rural fringe of towns and, in general, players of team games expect and are prepared to travel some distance to play. This is in contrast to young children or other regular users of open space who will usually hope to have informal open space or play features within easy reach of their homes.

Redevelopment of Existing Playing Fields

Many existing playing fields which were originally developed on the outskirts of towns have now been overtaken by development and occupy relatively expensive urban sites. Furthermore, because of changing patterns of sport, many of these playing fields are now used much less intensively and this increases the pressure to develop them for other uses. This is particularly the case with the playing fields provided by factories or other firms for their employees, and for school playing fields which are no

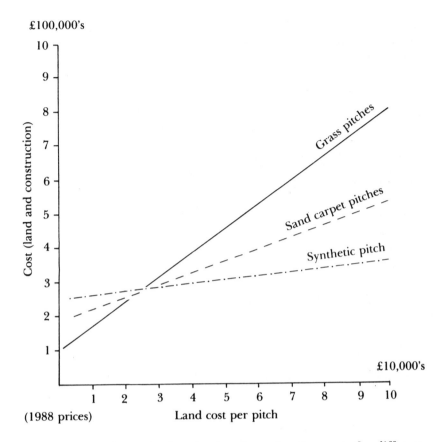

Figure 1.2   *The equivalent land and construction costs for different forms of pitch construction*

longer required because of falling school rolls or other demographic changes. In both cases, because of high land values, there are strong incentives either to redevelop the sites completely or to intensify the play onto a smaller area by constructing sand carpet or synthetic pitches.

Understandably these moves are usually resisted by local residents as well as the planning authorities, who are anxious to retain green spaces in otherwise developed areas. Opposition to development is frequently based on claims that there is a demand for the sports pitches but in many cases this is often not so and the case for retention has to rest on the desire for 'green prospects' and informal space for dog walking and general recreation.

Many of the existing playing fields are not particularly effective as 'amenity' areas. They are, almost by definition, flat, featureless and often bleak places providing little surface interest, shelter or changing scenery. Much smaller spaces, with well-designed planting and changes of level would be more effective in providing attractive scenery and pleasant recreation space and, at the same time, release some land for redevelopment. Unfortunately, these ideal schemes of partial development are difficult to achieve against the very persuasive influence of high land values and, as with many other developments, it is essential that the landscaping of the remaining land is made a binding commitment *before* the development is agreed.

Maintenance and Management Plans

Maintenance plans are an essential means of describing the regular maintenance operations, both for the purposes of discussing and agreeing on alternatives, and as a means of costing the work, either through 'in-house' arrangements or through competitive tendering. For most large sites, half a hectare upwards, a 1250 scale plan is usually sufficient to show the level of detail required and to provide a base for measuring off the quantities. In the first instance the base plans can be obtained from Ordnance Survey extracts but aerial survey plans will often give more detail of the features on site and therefore avoid extra surveying.

The maintenance regimes, gang-mowing, lawn mowing, shrub borders, etc. are usually colour-coded on the relevant areas of the plan. Although colour-coding is easy to read and understand, it is relatively expensive to produce and, in particular, cannot be easily photocopied or reproduced electronically. Therefore it may be preferable to use cross-hatching or other black-and-white coding methods where a large number of copy plans are likely to be needed.

The maintenance of fences and hedges and boundaries are

Site: *Bicton Old People's Home*   Date of survey/review: *March 1988*

Colour code	Description	Principal operations	Frequency/Season	Dimensions
Green	Lawns	Mow and box off	24/season	2600 m^2
		Mowing obstructions		27 obst.
		Edge clipping	10/season	315 m
		Spray mowing strips	1 Feb./March	94 m
		Re-cut kerb edges	1 Nov./Dec.	75 m
Hatched green	Rough grass and bulbs	Rotary mow	4 start mid-June	215 m^2
Red	Roses	Winter cultivation	1 Nov./Dec.	260 m^2
		Residual herbicide	1 Feb./March	260 m^2
		Dead-heading	3 July	260 m^2
		Autumn prune	1 Nov./Dec.	260 m^2
		Winter prune	1 Feb./March	260 m^2
		Spot weed	4 summer	260 m^2
Yellow	Shrubs	Winter cultivation	1 Nov./Dec.	506 m^2
		Residual herbicide	1 Feb./March	506 m^2
		Summer prune	1 June	50 m^2
		Winter prune	1 Nov.–Feb.	100 m^2
		Spot weed	4 summer	506 m^2
Brown	Ground Cover	Clip and tidy	1 winter	330 m^2
		Hand weed	4 summer	330 m^2
—	Young std. trees	Base spray	1 Feb./March	16 trees
		Check stakes and ties	2 autumn and spring	16 trees
A1	2 m beech hedge	Clip top and 2 sides	August	315 m^2
A2	1.5 m privet hedge	Clip top and 2 sides	3 May, June, Sept.	245 m^2
A3	Chain link fence	Base spray	1 Feb./March	145 m

Figure 1.3   *Example of a maintenance schedule*

more difficult to represent on the plan and so this generally has to be by number or letter coding of the different lengths of treatment and listing them on a schedule. Figure 1.3 gives an example of such a schedule and also shows the main areas and dimensions of the site. These dimensions are essential for producing precise contract documents, for bonus incentive schemes or for work planning.

Measuring the areas and lengths is a long and time-consuming task as each part of the site needs to be identified and measured separately even though it is only the overall totals that are needed for specification or pricing. In the past irregular-shaped areas could only be accurately measured by using a planimeter but, more recently, computer digitizing equipment has enabled measuring to be done by 'electronic pen'. However, if neither of these facilities is available, relatively close estimates can be made by placing a transparent scale grid over the plots and counting the unit areas. While these estimates could vary by as much as ± 10 per cent, they are accurate enough for most purposes, provided there is not a consistent bias above or below the mean.

Longer-term management plans are less frequently prepared for grounds maintenance, although they are regularly used for woodland management. A typical management plan is mainly composed of narrative with a map or plan to indicate the main areas or compartments of the site. The narrative then consists of a series of management events over the span of the plan, usually from 10 to 20 years although longer where there are significant areas of woodlands. This same approach can be useful for grounds maintenance and Figure 1.4 gives a typical example. The timespan for such a plan is best set at five years as this is a reasonable interval between regular reviews of the overall objectives, the levels of routine maintenance, and the need for non-regular events such as new or replacement planting.

The preparation of a management plan essentially goes through the process of surveying and recording what is present and then assessing the need or otherwise for altering the management regime or initiating layout or other changes. In practice, the initial recording can be a time-consuming exercise and may involve the collection of a lot of relatively unimportant data, e.g. the number and distribution of and approximate age of individual plant species. This information may be valued for detailed scientific monitoring but, in most circumstances, it is only necessary to record the basic facts that will identify the need for action or change. For example, if a shrub border is badly overgrown that fact is sufficient to signal radical pruning or replanting.

Site: *Bicton Park and Sports Ground*   Date of survey/review: *October 1987*

Area code	Description and condition	Proposed action	Year
1	N. E. shelter belt. Mixed deciduous. Overmature. 50 per cent Rhodo. cover.	Clear Rhodo's Selective fell and replant	88/89 89/90
2a	W. Tree screen. Young conifers	Thin by 25 per cent	90/91
2b	Newly planted broadleaves	Ring weed Formative pruning	88/90 90/91
3	Playing fields – ponding in lower corner	Renew main drain	90/91
4	Entrance drive and bulb meadow	Plant extra bulbs Reduce mowing to once a month	88/89 88/89
5	Walled garden. Run down herb. border on the west side	Refurbish w. border	88/89
6	Terrace and lawns. Poor and weedy growth	Fertilize and weedkill	89/90
7	Car park – breaking up on the main entrance	Mend pot holes	88/89
8	Courtyard and pond. Leaking? and overgrown	Clear, reline and replant	89/90
9	Paddock and lake. Starting to silt up	Dredge	92/93

Figure 1.4 *Site management plan*

In order to simplify the collection of the information it is essential to divide up any large site into simple sectors or compartments that can be easily identified and appreciated. The sectors can vary greatly in size as shown in Figure 1.4.

Once the management plan, or plans, have been completed, the necessary action can be formulated into a management programme as shown in Figure 1.5. This programme can then serve as a checklist and reminder for the manager or supervisors, and more importantly as a basis for annual budgeting. This process of budgeting may well indicate the need to reprogramme some of the projects to smooth both the costs and the staff workload.

The formal preparation of maintenance and management plans involves a considerable amount of professional time and

Year 88/89 Area code and project	Budget cost	Year 89/90 Area code and project	Budget cost	Year 90/91 Area code and project	Budget cost
1 Clear Rhodo's	£1200	1 Selective felling	£500	1 New plantings	£200
2b Ring weed new planting	£100	2b Ring weed new planting	£100	2a Thin conifers	£200
4 Plant extra bulbs	£400	7 Fertilise and weed kill main lawns	£300	2b Formative pruning	£50
5 Reduce mowing	£100 Credit	9 Reline pond and replant margins	£1800	3 Renew drainage system	£3000
6 Refurbish w. border	£1000				
8 Mend pot holes	£200				
TOTAL £2700		TOTAL £2700		TOTAL £3450	

Figure 1.5 *Management programme and draft budget*

expertise. For this reason they are often neglected but they are essential if the management style is to be anything more than managing by exception or in response to crisis or breakdown situations. Proper replanning is essential both to achieve the best use of our landscape resources and as a basis for the detailed supervision of the work, or the preparation of contract specifications that are dealt with in subsequent chapters.

Appendix 1.I

Cost-Benefit Implications of Playing Field Drainage

Assessing the Value of Drainage

The economic value of drainage on any plot of land is usually difficult to quantify in precise terms and even in agriculture, where crop yields can be accurately measured, it is still not possible to predict with any certainty what would be the most economic level of artificial drainage in terms of return on the capital involved. This does not mean that the advantages of drainage are not discernible but it does mean that it is very difficult to estimate the optimum level of capital investment. In sports field drainage the advantages are even more difficult to assess in economic terms and at best the capital costs can only be equated with matches played or not played or the numbers of days on which the surface is fit for use. Nevertheless, the costs of drainage can be considerable and it is important to attempt to predict what advantages could accrue from the installation of various alternative systems. This is particularly so when the performance of a drainage system can be accurately designed, using modern drainage techniques.

The advantages of playing field drainage are mainly that surface water (rainfall) is cleared more rapidly and the soil provides a better growing medium for the turf. These last advantages are often the most important in agriculture and include:

(a) earlier warming of the soil in spring
(b) earlier spring regeneration of worn turf
(c) improved drought resistance.

These improvements during the growing season can be considerable but during the winter months the more important effect of drainage is that rainfall is removed faster from the surface so that play can take place on a reasonably firm surface and without unduly damaging the soil structure. This increased availability for play is the factor on which most players would base their judgement on the value or otherwise of a drainage system.

How Much Drainage is Needed

The optimum drainage rate that a designer should try to achieve depends first on the rainfall that can be expected, and second on the proportion of lost playing days that the client is prepared to accept and the anticipated pattern of use.

Looking first of all at rainfall, Graph A.1 shows, as an example, how rainfall is likely to be distributed throughout the winter months. The graph is based on a ten-year period at a recording station in the south-east of England and shows that for half the days there was very little or no rain at all and only on about 20 days (11 per cent) in the whole winter was there more than 5 mm of rain. (Graphs from wetter parts of the country would show higher rainfalls but are likely to show a similar distribtion pattern.)

On the basis of this it is therefore possible that even a modest drainage rate would probably make a pitch playable for the majority of the time. However, with a low drainage rate it is likely that the heavy rain from the few really wet days would flood the surface for several days afterwards. Taking this last factor into account Graph A.2 has been constructed to show the likely number of lost days that can be expected with various levels of drainage capacity.

This again shows that for most of the time a relatively low drainage rate would be likely to keep the pitch clear and high drainage rates may only be needed for a very small number of days in any one year. Therefore, if the users can afford to be flexible in the way they use the pitches in winter and only use them when weather conditions are favourable, a relatively low drainage rate would be adequate. If, however, there is a strong user pressure to play on pitches whatever the weather, the drainage rate needs to be very much higher so that it will deal with most intensities of rain as it falls. A professional football club ground for instance probably comes within this category and here the necessary capital expenditure and maintenance of

Rainfall per day (mm)

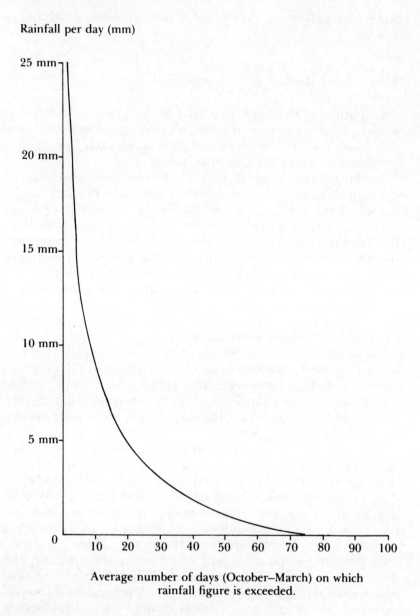

Average number of days (October–March) on which
rainfall figure is exceeded.

Graph A.1   *Average winter rainfall distribution*

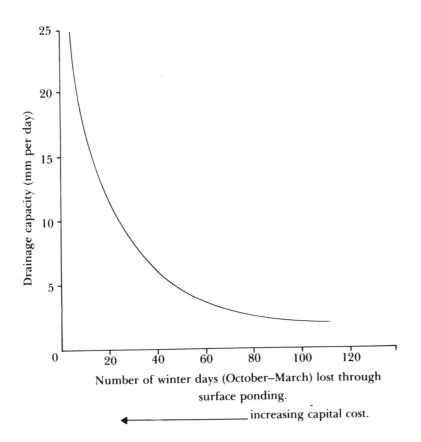

Graph A.2   *Theoretical relationship of days lost and drainage rate*

a high-intensity drainage system can usually be justified by fewer matches having to be cancelled. The figures in Graphs A.1 and A.2 both suggest the theoretical drainage requirements but in practice much higher rates are likely to be needed to take account of:

- local ponding in dips and hollows
- gradual deterioration of the drainage system (silting up, etc.)

- higher rainfall in wetter parts of the country, and
- year to year variations (when rainfall is above average).

Therefore, as a general guide a drainage rate of at least 25 mm a day is probably needed for even a lightly used winter pitch and at the other end of the scale a professional football pitch might require as much as 25 mm *per hour* if they are to be reasonably confident of staging their matches in all weathers. Such drainage rates can probably only be achieved with a rafted drainage system or a sand-based construction.

Drainage System and Design on Capital Cost

When sports field drainage systems are being designed there are often several different ways of achieving the same or similar end-results but the costs of the alternatives can sometimes be very different. In each situation the designer has to work out the likely cost difference and, for instance, decide between either a system of substantial surface slits and few underdrains or simple slits with many closely spaced interceptors.

The final best solution will depend on many factors, including the local availability of suitable materials, machinery and contractors, but the general principles given below should help as a guide towards achieving the lowest capital cost.

Spacing of Underground Laterals or Interceptor Drains

Underground laterals, with or without pipes, are nearly always more expensive to construct per metre than surface slits and for this reason alone it would appear sensible to use as few as possible. However, extra capital spent on underground laterals is usually more than amply repaid in drainage capacity and as a general rule a doubling of the number of underdrains will give a fourfold increase in the drainage rate.

Example: If laterals are laid 10 metres apart in a uniformly draining soil 0.5 metres deep with hydraulic conductivity of

1 cm/hr (.01 metres/hr), the drainage rate (based on Houg-houdt's simplified formula) will be

$$\frac{\cdot 5 \times \cdot 5 \times 4 \times \cdot 01}{10 \times 10}$$

= ·0001 metre/hr, or 0·1 mm/hr

If however the laterals were laid at 5-metre centres the drainage rate is

$$\frac{\cdot 5 \times \cdot 5 \times 4 \times \cdot 01}{5 \times 5}$$

= ·0004 metre/hr, or 0·4 mm/hr

This example shows the advantages of extra underground laterals but also illustrates that a misguided attempt to save capital cost by halving the number of laterals would reduce the drainage to a quarter of the original design rate.

This same principle will apply to the lower levels of any two or three-tier system of underground drains connecting with surface sand slits. It does not, however, apply to the top layer of slits that collect rain water directly from the surface.

Spacing of Surface Slits

Surface slits are usually relatively cheap per metre run but because they are close together, and many metres have to be laid, their total cost is a major part of the capital outlay. It is therefore often tempting to space them as widely apart as possible.

The scope for such saving is severely limited as surface slits only have an effective influence over a very narrow band, simply because rain water can only travel very slowly across the level surface of a playing field. Footmarks and the like will slow the surface flow down even more and in practice a surface slit will only drain a band about 1.5 metres wide. Thus even if slits are placed 2 metres apart there is a considerable risk of surface ponding or sogginess between the runs.

For this purely technical reason it is usually best to space surface slits at about a metre apart. Closer spacing will improve the drainage rate but the costs usually increase pro rata and it would normally be more economic to increase the number of underground drains.

Savings on surface slits can sometimes be made by only slitting the heavily used or badly drained parts of a pitch or field. Alternatively a whole pitch can be slit at 1.5 metre centres with additional slits put between to give .75 metre spacing on the wet or heavily used areas. (Note that this only gives a cost saving, compared with 1 metre spacing overall, if the wet areas are less than half of the total area.)

Comparisons of Alternative Systems

Some examples of possible costs of alternative systems are shown in Table A.1. The figures have been deliberately simplified in order to illustrate the comparisons and must only be used in that context. The availability of different materials and machinery could well alter the conclusions and in each case the designer must work out the costs that are likely to apply to the specific site.

Effect of Drainage on Total Use

All the above has been concerned with the effect of drainage rates on the chances of pitches being water-logged at any one time and does not take account of the total hours of use of the surface once drainage problems have been eliminated. This total use is normally limited by the amount of wear that the actual surface carpet of turf is able to bear. Improved drainage will influence this to the extent that it encourages better growth and also that a drier surface discourages the players from sliding and damaging the turf by a shearing action. However, the more important effect of adequate drainage is to make a pitch playable throughout the season and allow considerably more play in the wettest months of the winter, as without drainage the pitch could be completely unplayable for weeks on end.

Table A.1 *Examples of slit drainage systems with a design rate of 48 mm/day (2 mm/hr)*

Scheme	Laterals spaced at	Surface slits Dimensions	Spacing	Filled with	Approx. cost per hectare* Laterals	Slits	Total
Ideal schemes							
a	22 m	60 × 300 mm	1 m	fine gravel and sand top	£1140	£10,000	£11,140
b	4.7 m	60 × 300 mm	1 m	medium sand	£5320	£6000	£11,320
c	6.6 m	60 × 300 mm	0.5 m	medium sand	£3790	£12,000	£15,790
Cost-cutting schemes							
d	18 m	60 × 300 mm	1.5 m	fine gravel and sand top	£1400	£6700	£8100
e	3.8 m	60 × 300 mm	1.5 m	medium sand	£6580	£4000	£10,580

*Estimated 1981 prices excluding mains, outlets, junctions, etc.: Laterals @ £2.50 per metre, Sand top/gravel slits @ £1 per metre, Sand only slits @ £0.6 per metre.

Notes: 1. Little to choose between a and b, but b has the advantage that, even without the slits, the underground laterals would give a fair measure of drainage if the field was lightly used and retained a good surface structure.
2. c has the same advantage as b but the extra cost of the close slits is unlikely to be justified except on very heavily used areas; goal mouths, etc.
3. d is significantly cheaper but wider slit spacing would be less effective under heavy use.
4. e has only a slight cost advantage and would not normally be worth considering.
5. a and d could be upgraded to a design rate of 8 mm *per hour* by doubling the number of underground laterals at an extra capital cost of only around £1200–£1400.

Cost Saving Strategy for a New Playing Field

Artificial drainage is only necessary when the natural drainage is inadequate, but when a new playing field is being planned it is extremely difficult to assess, in advance, what the natural drainage rate will be. Soil structure can easily be destroyed by adverse weather conditions during levelling and grading, or merely by the time the top soil stays in the stack.

Once a field is sown down the natural soil structure may regenerate again within a year or two on heavy clays by the natural expansion and contraction of the clay particles through the seasons. On silty soils, however, the natural structure, once lost, may not reform for very many years. Therefore depending on soil types an elaborate and expensive drainage system could be of only temporary value or an absolute essential in the long term.

In order to minimize the risks of either extreme it would be wise only to lay a basic underdrainage system during the construction stage. Subsequently a slit drainage system can be added at a later date if it is found necessary, either across the whole field or across the goal mouths or any special wet areas. (See, for example, schemes a and b in Table A.1, where the major capital cost could at least be delayed until experience proved the full slit system was needed.) In this way the capital costs can be kept to a minimum but there are often administrative difficulties with obtaining an additional capital sum for sand slitting several years after the main part of the construction has been completed. It is therefore essential to ensure that the promoters of the construction scheme are aware of the possible need for extra works as the new playing field becomes established.

Finally, it cannot be over-emphasized that any drainage system will be largely wasted if it is not backed up by regular maintenance, not only to prevent pore blockage and smearing of sand slits, but also to retain as open a soil structure as possible.

Chapter 2

ROUTINE MAINTENANCE AND SITE HUSBANDRY

The regular care and maintenance of any area of landscape has a profound affect on its appearance, its value as an amenity and, even in the longer term, its plant communities and overall nature. The right levels of maintenance, and the methods to be used, will vary considerably from site to site and as well as being influenced by the layout and use, will also be a reflection of the soil types, topography, exposure to the elements and local climatic variations.

Matching the maintenance regimes to the needs of a site is a major part of the art and science of landscape management and it is not possible to give any absolute prescription or standard specification that can be applied for a particular type of landscape. However, this chapter attempts to describe and define the main operations that go into routine maintenance together with some indication of the labour that they are likely to take. Under the heading of each main type of landscape feature there are some introductory notes on the management considerations and then performance specifications or objectives for the various operations.

The times that are given against the operations have mostly been derived from work study-based bonus incentive schemes and therefore assume a working rate equivalent to standard performance (see Chapter 5). However, the times, mostly given as a range, can only be regarded as a guide in the absence of a very detailed specification appropriate to the site and working practices.

The specifications and operations are grouped under the following headings:

Grassland and sports turf
Fine turf, golf greens, cricket squares, etc.
Playing fields, rugby, football, hockey.
Lawns
Low maintenance swards, verges, meadowland, etc.
Shrub borders
Ground cover
Rose borders
Herbaceous borders
Annual bedding
Hedges
Newly planted trees
Hard paved surfaces
General litter clearance

Finally, in Appendix 2.I, a list of seasonal work hours is given for some of the same landscape features.

Grassland – General

Amenity grassland has become the generic term for all natural and semi-natural grassland used for recreation purposes as distinct from that used for productive agriculture. It forms the major part of the landscape and its maintenance takes up more man hours during the summer growing season (see Figure 2.1) than any other activity.

Grassland types can be divided into five broad categories depending upon intended use and management. The most expensive to maintain are the intensively used, highly specialized sports turfs found on golf greens, tennis courts, cricket tables and bowling greens. The grasses which form the turf need to be specially selected and highly tolerant of the extreme conditions under which they are grown and used; inputs such

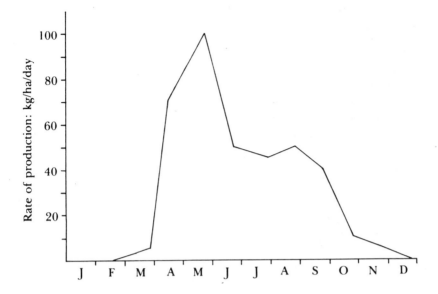

Figure 2.1   *A typical growth pattern for grassland in lowland England*

as carefully controlled mowing, fertilizing, herbicides and fungicide treatments need to be carried out with skill and correct timing to maintain the necessary balance and produce a quality surface.

Turf for winter games areas such as football, hockey and rugby constitute a second category of intensively maintained turf.[1] While to produce high-quality pitches, particularly during the winter months, is no less demanding than for the previous category, the margins for error are greater, areas are larger and mowing costs less.

General grass areas around homes and public buildings form the third category. Maintenance inputs need not be high and the demands of keeping the turf to a reasonable standard are not excessive. The design of this type of lawn is critical, the main maintenance input is mowing and the smaller and more irregular, or steeper the area, the greater the mowing cost. As costs rise the use of alternative groundcover e.g. shrubs or the use of growth retardant chemicals need to be actively considered.

The fourth category comprises non-intensively used areas such as highway verges and maintenance objectives are limited to keeping the vegetation to a defined height.

'Natural' grassland such as wildflower meadows make different demands on management. Unlike the intensively-used turf which relies on a limited range of specialised cultivars the objective is to produce a diverse sward. This requires carefully applied maintenance techniques and is not always the 'cheap' alternative sometimes advocated, but it does have the advantage of reducing peak workloads.

The range of machines used to maintain grassland is wide, commencing at the hand scythe or hook, and progressing through powered strimmers, flails, rotary mowers, gang-mowers to cylinder mowers of increasing sophistication. It is important to ensure the best match between mower and desired end-result. For instance, flail mowers would not produce a bowling green and cylinder mowers are not appropriate to maintain roadside verges.

Apart from mowing there are a number of common operations involved in the maintenance of intensively used turf, i.e. spiking, scarifying, top dressing, herbicide and pesticide treatment, fertilizing, etc., the frequency and intensity of which will vary. However mowing, of all management practices, is the most important in producing the kind of turf required for a particular use.

Detailed specifications for sports surfaces are now being developed by the Sports Council and others, in terms of ball bounce and travel as well as surface traction and smoothness. The detail of these is outside the scope of this book and rely as much, if not more, on the soil or substrate composition as on the maintenance of the vegetation which is specified here. Even the maintenance of the grass in fine turf is a whole subject in its own right and the groundsman's skill is tested to the limits on the first-class wickets and greens that the sports require. It is not possible to cover all aspects of this work in this book but the main routine operations are included.

Fine Turf – Cricket Squares

Maintenance objective

To provide a level consolidated surface, free of stones, dichoty-ledenous weeds and surface irregularities covered with an even thatch-free stand of grass on which can be prepared individual cricket wickets.

Maintenance operations

(a) The grass shall be maintained between 6–10 mm during the period April to September and 10–20 mm for the rest of the year. (To achieve this will require mowing up to twice and perhaps three times in a seven-day period with cuttings removed – 56 hours/year per cricket square.)

(b) The surface shall be consolidated to a depth of 100 mm by the use of rollers of increasing weight when soil conditions are suitable. Minimum 10 hours per year.

(c) The sward shall be kept weed-free by the use of approved herbicides (2 hours per year) and actively growing by the application of fertilisers (3 hours per year) in split applications to provide 75 kg N/ha, 30 kg P/ha and 75 kg K/ha.

(d) The sward shall be thoroughly scarified at the end of the playing season to ensure that the soil surface is free of dead organic matter (14 hours per cricket square).

(e) The surface shall be spiked to a depth of not less than 100 mm at the end of the playing season to reduce compaction (3 hours). In addition, surface spiking to a depth of 10 mm to permit water penetration shall be carried out monthly in the playing season.

(f) Worms and other pests, e.g. leatherjackets, shall be eliminated from the square using an approved pesticide (4 hours per year).

(g) Worn areas shall be re-seeded using an approved seed mixture generally containing 80 per cent. Chewings fescue and 20 per cent Browntop Bent or up to 30 per cent approved turf type perennial ryegrass (three hours).

(h)   At the end of the season the square shall be top dressed using a heavy binding soil with a clay content of greater than 25 per cent (10 hours per cricket square). This operation may be carried out only once in every two or three years, according to the class of cricket being played, but is highly desirable as an annual operation for good class squares.

Winter brushing may also be of benefit (see p. 39–(g)).

Grass Tennis Courts

Maintenance objective

To provide a firm, level surface free of irregularities and weeds on which the ball will achieve a true bounce and not be deviated from the intended line.

Maintenance operations

(a)   The turf should be maintained to a height of between 6 mm and 8 mm with clippings boxed off. Mowing during peak growth periods should be two or three times per week (1 hour per week per court).

(b)   The court should be firmed after the winter by the use of a roller weighing 250–500 kg (2 hours).

(c)   The turf should be maintained in active growth by the application of fertilizers to provide the equivalent of 75 kg N, 30 kg P and 75 kg K per hectare in split applications (2 hours per year).

(d)   Thatch should be kept to the minimum to prevent the development of a 'slow' court by regular light scarification. However, at least one annual scarify is essential (two hours per court per occasion).

(e)   At the end of the playing season the court should be spiked to a depth of at least 100 mm to reduce compaction and improve aeration (3 hours).

(f)   The court shall be kept weed- and pest-free by the application of appropriate chemicals (2–6 hours per year).

(g)   At the end of the season the court should be top dressed with a medium binding soil – clay content approximately 20 per cent – to preserve levels (four hours). (Not essential every year but desirable on good quality courts.)

The court should be brushed during the winter period to disperse worm casts (one hour per court per occasion; say, five times per year).

Bowling Greens (Flat)

Maintenance objective

To provide a dense close mown substantially thatch-free turf surface which is even and over which the bowls will run smoothly. The maximum surface irregularity should be 6 mm under a 2 m straight edge and a bowl should cover the distance to the jack (27.4 m) in 10–12 seconds.

Maintenance operations

(a)   Mowing shall be carried out to maintain the grass to between 6 mm and 8 mm. (This will require up to three cuts in seven days and perhaps on high quality greens five cuts in seven days.) The direction of cut shall be varied on each cut to avoid grain. Clippings shall be boxed off (75–105 hours per year per green). Brush prior to mowing (40–60 hours).

(b)   Rolling will be required to refirm the green after the winter using a roller weighing 250–500 kg (6 hours per green).

(c)   Rolling with a 'true level' roll to smooth the surface weekly to be carried out. Scarification will be required at the end of the season to remove excessive thatch which will slow the green (30 hours).

(d)   Top dressing with an appropriate sand/soil mix to correct any irregularities (20 hours).

(e) If surface levels are uneven hollow tine spike (10 hours), lightly roll (two hours) and top dress (20 hours).

(f) During the playing season the surface should be spiked to 10 mm using a sarrol roller (2 hours).

(g) The green shall be kept moss- and weed-free using approved chemicals (4 hours per green per year).

(h) The green shall be fertilized to provide the equivalent of 100 kg N, 30 kg P and 100 kg K per hectare in split applications (10 hours per year).

(i) The green shall be treated with approved fungicides as preventative treatments (8 hours per year).

Golf Greens

Maintenance objective

To provide a dense closely-mown grass surface on which the golf ball will not be deviated from the chosen line by the grass.

Maintenance operations

(a) The grass shall be maintained between 5 and 8 mm and mowing will be required up to 3–5 times per week. Mowing shall be carried out in different directions on each cut to avoid the creation of 'grain' (78–126 hours per year per green). The green can be brushed prior to mowing (12 hours per year).

(b) Rolling will be required to firm the surface following winter using a roller weighing between 250 and 500 kg (3 hours).

(c) The green should be regularly but lightly scarified to ensure that thatch does not build up and that the putting surface is not damaged (18 hours per year).

(d) The green should be top dressed annually with an appropriate sand/soil mix to correct any minor surface irregularities and to assist in the control of thatch (8 hours).

(e) The flagstick shall be moved regularly up to weekly to avoid excessive wear on the green (12 hours per year).

(f) The green shall be spiked weekly using a sarrol roller to improve aeration and water penetration (28 hours per year).

(g) The green shall be kept moss- and weed-free by the application of approved pesticides (2 hours per year).

(h) The green shall be kept free of fungal pathogens and insect pests by the use of appropriate pesticides (6 hours per year).

(i) The green shall be fertilized to provide the equivalent of 100 kg N, 30 kg P and 100 kg K per hectare in split applications (4 hours per year).

Hockey Pitches

Maintenance objective

To provide a level, even surface covered by a dense sward of grass substantially free of broadleaved weeds. The surface should allow a hockey ball to run true for a minimum of 25 m after being struck by a player.

Maintenance operations

(a) The grass shall be maintained to a height of 25–50 mm between April and August using a gang-mower (5 hours per year).

(b) From August to March (or the end of the playing season) maintain the grass at a height of 15–25 mm and remove the arisings. Only pedestrian operated or other light machinery that will not mark the surface of the pitch shall be used (allow 70 hours per year per pitch).

(c) Keep the sward substantially weed-free by the use of an approved selective herbicide (2 hours per year).

(d) Maintain satisfactory turf growth by the application of fertilizer to supply 45 kg N/ha, 10 kg P/ha and 45 kg K/ha (2 hours per year).

(e) During the playing season maintain a true level surface, particularly in the shooting areas, by regular brushing, dragmatting or light rolling (42 hours per year).

(f)   The pitch should be spiked to a depth of at least 100 mm during appropriate weather conditions to allow penetration of water (say 6 times a year, 1–2 hours per occasion using a tractor mounted spiker).

(g)   Pitches shall be marked out in accordance with the current laws of the game and all markings shall be in white and clearly visible for all competitive games, i.e. clearly visible from 20 metres at right angles to the line. (16 hours per year assuming weekly marking.)

(h)   Goal posts shall be erected and taken down as required and painted white (3 hours per year).

(i)   Goal mouth areas shall be spiked and dressed with sand as required to ensure a firm, dry foothold (10 hours per year).

(j)   After each match, but at least once per week, divots shall be replaced or, where this is not practical, the depressions caused shall be top dressed with a sand/soil mix (40 hours per year).

Football Pitches

Maintenance objective

To provide a level true surface covered with a dense growth of grass. The surface should be free of irregularities that would deflect the ball from its intended direction.

Maintenance operations

(a)   Maintain the height of the grass to between 20 mm and 50 mm high. Clippings can be allowed to fly (20 hours per year per pitch).

(b)   The sward should be maintained substantially weed free by the application of an appropriate selective herbicide (2 hours per year per pitch).

(c)   Active grass growth should be promoted by the application of fertilizer to provide 45 kg N, 10 kg P and 45 kg K per hectare (2 hours per year).

(d)   The surface should be smoothed by brushing, harrowing

or rolling with a light roller once per week (total time 22 hours).

(e) During the playing season the pitch should be spiked when weather conditions are suitable to a depth of at least 100 mm (allow for up to 9 times giving a total of 12 hours).

(f) The goal mouth area should be spiked by hand and top dressed with sand to ensure a firm dry surface (10 hours per year).

(g) The pitch should be marked in accordance with the laws of the game and all markings maintained clearly visible, i.e. at 20 metres at right-angles to the line (20 hours per year).

(h) Goal posts should be painted annually and erected and taken down at the start and end of the season and stored safely (3 hours per year).

Rugby Pitches

Maintenance objective

To provide a level surface covered with a dense layer of grass to absorb the impact of falling players.

Maintenance operations

(a) From August to March, maintain the grass to a height of between 50 mm and 100 mm leaving the clippings to fly. During the remainder of the year the grass can be cut to a height of 20 mm to 50 mm for summer sports or maintained at 50 mm–100 mm (12 hours per year).

(b) To enable line marking to be carried out the grass in the areas to be marked shall be maintained at a height of 20–50 mm (19 hours per year).

(c) The sward should be kept generally weed-free (not more than 10 per cent weed cover in any area) by the application of an approved selective weedkiller (2 hours).

(d) Fertilizer should be applied in one or more applications to provide 45 kg N, 10 kg P and 45 kg K per hectare (3 hours).

(e)   The pitch area should be spiked to a depth of at least 100 mm to ensure infiltration of water, on up to three occasions (3 hours per occasion).

(f)   Pitch renovation after games should be allowed for to repair the damage caused by scrummages, etc. (1 hour per occasion).

(g)   Prior to the start of the season the pitch should be set out in accordance with the laws of the game and lines maintained clearly visible thereafter (20 hours per season).

(h)   Posts should be erected and removed at the start and finish of the playing season. Prior to storage they should be rubbed down and given one good coat of white paint (6 hours).

General Amenity Grass Areas

Maintenance objective

To provide an even stand of vegetation of uniform height and colour comprising predominantly grass species, although a small percentage of dichotyledenous plants – no more than 5 per cent – would be acceptable.

Maintenance operations

(a)   Mowing shall be carried out using a cylinder mower to maintain the vegetation length within the limits of 20 mm and 40 mm during April to August inclusive and between 30 mm and 50 mm during the rest of the year. (This will normally require mowing at up to once a week in the peak of the season, say, 20 times per year.)
      The clippings shall be let fly but must be distributed evenly over the surface and at no time shall the layer of clippings be of such a depth that will affect the growth of vegetation (15–21 hours per year per 1000m^2).

Additional operations:

(a)   The clippings may be boxed off and the vegetation kept to between 15 and 30 mm during April to August and 20–40 mm during the rest of the year (22–24 hours per year).

(b) All edges of grass areas, against buildings, footpaths, roadways, trees, posts and any other obstruction shall be kept neat and tidy (2 hours per year per 100 linear metres).

(c) Mowing strips against walls, etc. shall be 150 mm wide and may be maintained by the use of an appropriate herbicide (1 hour per year per 100 linear metres).

(d) Border edges shall be clipped and not be allowed to exceed 50 mm length (11 hours per year per 100 linear metres).

(e) Grass areas may be sprayed overall with a suitable approved selective herbicide in accordance with the manufacturer's instructions. Alternatively, spot weeding of isolated weed infestation may be carried out (1 hour per year per 1000 m²).

(f) Fertilizers may be applied in the period March to September to provide 40 kg N, 10 kg P and 40 kg K per hectare (1 hour per year). (Only necessary for formal areas.)

(g) Reinstatement by re-turfing or re-seeding of worn areas may be undertaken as necessary.

Meadow Areas

Maintenance objective

To maintain a species rich sward appropriate to the soil type of the site – or to the locality if the soil is non-natural.

Maintenance operations

(a) The vegetation shall be cut as appropriate to encourage the perpetuation of the desired species mix in either late June or early July, followed by a second cut in late August or early September, or a single cut late in

September. In both cases all cut vegetation shall be removed off site (3–4 hours per hectare for mowing per occasion).

Additional operations:

  (a) Spot treatment of noxious weeds using selective herbicide (6 hours per hectare).

Rough Grass

Maintenance objective

To maintain an even cover of long vegetation and to control undesirable dicotyledenous species, e.g. dock, thistle, ragwort, nettles, etc.

Maintenance operations

  (a) The vegetation shall be cut once per year in September to December to reduce herbage to 100 mm (3–10 hours per year per hectare). Alternatively, two cuts may be carried out, the first in late June/early July to control the early flush of growth.

Additional operations:

  (a) Spot treatment of noxious weeds using selective herbicide.

Shrub Borders – General

Shrub borders are often the mainstay of formal ornamental landscapes and building surrounds. For cost-effective maintenance the aim should be to achieve a closely covering boscage over the whole surface of the soil, preferably of shrubs that require little regular pruning to provide their ornamental effect (flowers, foliage, autumn colour, etc.). Once established such borders are cheaper to maintain per unit area, than small lawns and require very little attention through the growing season.

Weed control and cultivations, if any, need only be carried out on the visible soil surface.

Treatment during the first 5–10 years after planting is critical. The borders must be kept weed-free, particularly of perennial weeds, with close planting to give early cover. However, the plants must be thinned rigorously so that the shrubs that are retained are able to achieve an attractive form. This may involve removing the intermediate plants as soon as the shoots are touching.

Once established, the plants should not need major replanting for at least 20 years or so, although earlier replanting may often be necessary in building surrounds where large shrubs start to overgrow paths or block light to windows.

The most difficult management task is to achieve a sensitive and consistent programme of pruning. Carefully designed borders will need little regular pruning and attention once in two years by skilled operatives should be sufficient.

Maintenance objective

Maintain a boscage of shrub growth to cover as much as possible of the border area and allowing the individual plants to achieve as nearly as possible their natural form. Maintain the borders free of visible weeds and shape and prune the shrubs to avoid obstructing pathways or blocking light to windows.

Maintenance operations: Newly planted borders

(a) Immediately after planting and thereafter yearly, in appropriate season for the species involved, prune the shrubs to develop their desirable ornamental characteristics. At the same time remove intermediate plants that are restricting the natural and attractive development of their neighbours. Remove all arisings from site (1–3 hours per 100 m^2).

(b) Lightly cultivate the surface soil, to a depth of approximately 100 mm, remove or bury all annual weed or

Watering 0.5 – 1 hr per 100m^2 transplanted pump 10 litres per 100m^2.

natural litter and break any surface capping. Take special care to avoid unnecessary damage to the shrub plants and ensure that all the shrubs are firmly bedded in the soil. Leave the surface with a fine and even tilth with soil crumbs of less than 50 mm in diameter. Once a year operation in early winter (November/December) (3–5 hours per 100 m²).

Note: This operation is only essential where the soil is compacted or as a means of incorporating mulch. It does, however, make the surface of a newly planted bed look much more attractive while the plants are young and/or through the winter months. Not required where the borders are mulched.

(c) Maintain the soil surface substantially free of weeds (less than 5 per cent weed cover) by applying an annual dressing of Simazine, or approved equivalent, residual herbicide in the winter months and spot treating with Glyphosate, Dichlobenil, or approved equivalent, or removing any emergent weeds during the growing season. (Simazine application 0.3–0.5 hours per 100 m². Spot treatment at approximately four-weekly intervals in the main growing season, say five times per season. 0.1–0.3 hours per 100 m² per occasion.)

Note: As an alternative the borders can be regularly hand-hoed at up to two-weekly intervals in the main growing season, say six times per year (1–2 hours per 100 m² per occasion). This procedure is often recommended for the first one or two years after planting when the plants may be more sensitive to herbicide damage.

(d) Immediately after planting or, when subsequently directed, mulch the surface of the border with a 75 mm layer of coarse peat, pulverised bark (maximum particle size 40 mm), or other approved equivalent. Thereafter, top dress the mulch as necessary and at least once a year to maintain effective cover. Spot treat or remove any emergent weeds as specified in (c) above but do not cultivate or incorporate the mulch into the soil. (Initial application 1–2 hours per 100 m², spot treatment 0.1–0.3 hours per 100 m² per occasion.)

Note: The cost of the mulch usually makes this an expensive though effective alternative. (Probably at least five times more than just using residual herbicides.) However, the shrubs may show improved growth in response to the mulch.

Maintenance operations: Established borders

(a) Prune the shrubs as much as is necessary to achieve their desirable ornamental features (flowering, autumn colours, etc.), and to prevent them overgrowing footpaths or blocking light to windows. Remove all arisings from site as well as any damaged dead or diseased parts of the shrub (1–3 hours per 100 m^2).

(b) Cultivate any surface soil that is visible, as specified for newly planted borders (three to five hours per 100 m^2 of visible soil surface).
    Note: Only necessary in very formal areas.

(c) Maintain any visible surface soil free of weeds as specified for newly planted borders (Simazine application 0.3–0.5 hours per 100 m^2, spot treatment, up to five times per season, 0.1–0.3 hours per 100 m^2, both for visible soil surface only).

Ground Cover – General

Dense, low-growing plants, usually shrubs, which cover the ground and smother any weeds. Once established they need very little regular care and are therefore cheaper to maintain than small lawns per unit of area. They can be decorative in their own right, e.g. Hypericum sp. or low-growing roses, but they are particularly useful for clothing banks or other areas where grass mowing would be difficult.

Ground-cover needs careful establishment, i.e. during the first two or three years to ensure that any perennial weeds are eliminated. Plantings have a relatively short life and depending on the species, may need to be replaced after 10 to 15 years.

Maintenance objective:

Maintain a dense, weed-free cover of healthy growth, clipped or pruned as necessary to give a neat and tidy finish and contained within the planted area.

Maintenance operations:

   (a) Maintain the area substantially free of weeds (less than 5 per cent of weed cover) by applying an annual dressing of Simazine, or approved equivalent residual herbicide in the winter months and removing or spot treating any emergent weeds during the growing season with Glyphosate Dichlobenil, or approved equivalent. (Simazine application 0.3–0.5 hours per 100 m^2). Not likely to be needed after the first two years after planting. (Spot treatment or weed removal at approximately four-weekly intervals in the main growing season say five times per year, 0.1–0.3 hours per 100 m^2 per occasion. Frequency to drop, as the plants establish, down to once a year.)

   (b) Trim and tidy the plants once a year in the winter months, to remove dead vegetation or overgrowing branches. Remove all arisings from site (0.5–1.0 hours per 100 m^2. The amount of work will vary according to the species and may be reduced to once in two years for established borders.)

Rose Borders – General

Rose borders are relatively easy to cultivate and provide a reliable way of providing bright and attractive flowers during the summer months. The labour requirements are relatively even throughout the whole year (provided weed control is by herbicide or mulch), but the costs per unit area are likely to be significantly higher than for shrub borders.

Major replanting of rose borders may be necessary about once every 15 years although many may survive satisfactorily for rather longer.

Species roses need rather different treatment to the hybrid tea or floribunda roses and are therefore usually dealt with as a shrub border.

Maintenance objective

Maintain a free-flowering border of healthy hybrid tea or floribunda roses (or other equivalents) by regular pruning and fertilizing, in a weed-free border and substantially free from summer pests and diseases. Remove dead flowers in season so that all the dead heads are removed within two weeks of petal drop.

Optional extras

Lightly cultivate the soil surface in early autumn to remove soil capping and bury leaves and other surface litter. Or, top dress the soil surface in early autumn by adding a 75 mm layer of bark mulch, well-rotted compost or similar approved material.

Maintenance operations

   (a)   Top prune the roses to approximately two-thirds of their height in the autumn and remove the cuttings from site (one operation only, November/December, 2.5–3 hours per 100 m^2).
   (b)   Hard prune the roses to 150–300 mm from ground level according to type and vigour in the late winter. Cut to outward facing buds and then remove prunings from site (one operation only, February, 2.5–3.5 hours per 100 m^2).
   (c)   Supply and spread a 7:7:7 granular fertilizer or approved equivalent at 30 g/m^2 (one operation only in February/March. 0.1–0.2 hours per 100 m^2).
   (d)   Lightly cultivate the surface soil, to a depth of approximately 150 mm, remove or bury all annual weed or natural surface litter and break any surface capping. Take special care to avoid unnecessary damage to the roots of the rose plants and ensure that all the roses are firmly bedded in the ground. Leave the surface with a

fine and even tilth with soil crumbs of less than 50 mm
diameter (one operation only in the early winter,
November/December, 3–5 hours per 100 m^2).

Note: This operation is not essential (unless the soil is
compacted or as a means of incorporating mulch) but
will radically improve the appearance of the beds in the
winter months and leave them ready and clean for a
residual herbicide application.

(e) Maintain the soil surface substantially free of weeds (less
than 5 per cent weed cover) by applying an annual
dressing of Simazine, or approved equivalent, in the
winter months and spot treating, with Glyphosate, Dichlobenil, or approved equivalent, or removing any emergent weeds at least once every four weeks throughout the
growing season. (Simazine application 0.3–0.5 hours per
100 m^2, spot treatment at approximately four-weekly
intervals in the main growing season, say five times per
season, 0.1–0.3 hours per 100 m^2 per occasion.)

(f) Remove all dead flower heads within two weeks of petal
fall ('dead head'). Allow for carrying out this operation
up to three times per season (1–2 hours per 100 m^2).

(g) Keep the borders substantially free of sucker growths
(less than 5 per cent of the plants to have sucker growths
of more than 200 mm high) by removing all the growths
at regular intervals. Allow for clearing at least twice per
season (0.5–1.5 hours per 100 m^2).

(h) Keep the plants substantially free of fungal disease and
aphids (less than 20 per cent for the leaf or shoots
infected) by regular spraying with a Benomyl and Pyr-
ethrins mixture or approved equivalent. Allow for up to
three sprays per season (0.3–0.5 hours per 100 m^2, using
a knapsack sprayer).

Herbaceous Borders – General

Herbaceous borders are a relatively rare feature in parks and
public open spaces, probably because of their need for regular
care through the growing months and the associated expense.

Weedy or poorly maintained borders can be very unsightly but well-designed and cultivated borders are extremely attractive and an adequate reward for the labour and expense. Therefore, if herbaceous borders are to be maintained, they need to be grown properly without any half measures.

With careful selection of species and cultivars, it is possible to achieve a relatively inexpensive form of ground cover which gives much more seasonal variation and variety of colour and form than the conventional shrubby ground cover.

Maintenance objective

Maintain the herbaceous border in an attractive and free-flowering state, with the plants supported as necessary to achieve their full flowering form and kept substantially free of weeds, unattractive dead flowers, or diseased and damaged shoots.

Maintenance operations

(a) Cut down and remove all the dead shoots, as soon as possible after the first autumn frosts, and lightly cultivate the soil, to a depth of at least 150 mm to bury weeds and surface litter and break up surface compaction. Also dig, divide and replant in accordance with good horticultural practice to maintain a full cover of plants throughout the border (3–5 hours per 100 m^2).

(b) In the late spring, apply a 7:7:7 granular fertilizer, or approved equivalent at the rate of 30 g per m^2 to the surface of the border and lightly work it into the soil by hoeing (0.3–0.5 hours per 100 m^2). This fertilizer may be supplemented, or replaced, by a winter mulch of farm yard manure or similar (1–2 hours per 100 m^2 for spreading but excluding delivery to the site).

(c) Regularly hand hoe the visible soil surface to keep it free of weeds over 50 mm high. Allow for hoeing at up to once in two weeks in the main growing season, say six times per year (1–2 hours per 100 m^2).

Note: As an alternative, weed control can be achieved

by application of Lenacil herbicide at 6–10-week intervals.

(d) Regularly stake and tie or support the growing plants, using pea sticks or canes so that plants and flower heads are sufficiently stable in wind and rain. Allow for staking and tying at two-week intervals in the main growing season, say six times per year. (0.5–1 hour per 100 m^2).

(e) Remove unsightly dead flower heads within two weeks of petal fall. Allow for this operation up to five times per season (1–1.5 hours per 100 m^2).

Annual Bedding – General

Annual bedding requires considerable horticultural skill, both in the choice and production of the plants and in their subsequent care. Although it is scorned by some commentators, it is often well appreciated by the public in town centres and formal parks. It is generally inappropriate in informal or rural surroundings and because of its high cost it should usually be restricted to those areas where it will have the most impact.

Maintenance objective

Provide attractive flowering displays in at least two seasons of the year by planting out and cultivating, annuals, biennials, bulbs and other flowering plants as specified or provided.

Maintenance operations

(a) At the end of the flowering season, remove all the remaining plants and bulbs and dig over the bed to a depth of at least 250 mm to bury all surface litter and annual weeds and leave the soil with a fine tilth suitable for planting (3–5 hours per 100 m^2).

(b) Immediately after digging, apply a 7:7:7 granular fertilizer or approved equivalent, at 30 g/m^2 and lightly work it into the surface of the soil (0.3–0.5) hours per 100 m^2).

Note: This may be supplemented or replaced by spreading a liberal (5 m^3/100 m^2) dressing of farmyard manure or similar to the surface before the digging over in (a) above 1–2 hours per 100 m^2 excluding transport to the site).

(c) As soon as possible after clearing and cultivation, plant up the border with the plants, bulbs or corms as specified at the dimensions shown on the planting plan. Ensure that all the plants are properly and neatly firmed into the soil and, if necessary, thoroughly moisten the soil to a depth of at least 150 mm. Allow for twice a year (0.5–1 hour per 100 plants and excluding any watering).

(d) Throughout the winter months regularly hand-hoe the surface soil to break the surface crust and remove weeds, and pick off and remove any dead or diseased leaves on the plants. Allow for this operation at six-weekly intervals in suitable weather conditions, say four times per winter season (2–3 hours per 100 m^2).

(e) Throughout the growing season keep the soil free from visible weeds by regular hoeing. Pick off and remove any dead or diseased leaves or shoots of the cultivated plants. Allow for this operation at up to two weekly intervals through the growing season (say six times per season) (2–3 hours per 100 m^2).

Hedges – General

Hedges are a valuable asset in amenity areas, providing screening and shelter as well as privacy and protection. However, the costs of upkeep can be considerable depending on the height and length of the hedge, and plant species and the degree of formality that is required. In recent years the development of tractor-mounted flail hedge-cutters has radically reduced the costs, where tractor access is possible, both by speeding up the cutting process and so finely chopping the arisings that there is little need to clear up afterwards.

Where hedges are on property boundaries, there needs to be a measure of cooperation between the neighbouring owners for the regular maintenance, either to share the labour of cutting or allow access for the owner to do it.

Careful clipping and pruning during the early years after planting is very important in order to develop a well-clothed hedge.

Maintenance objective

Regularly clip the hedge to maintain a uniform and tidy appearance (according to the type of hedge and situation) and a well-developed cover of vegetation over the whole of the hedge surface. Regularly mow or otherwise control any weed or grass growth at the base of the hedge so that it does not detract from the overall appearance.

Maintenance operations

(a) Clip the top and sides of the hedge to maintain true and even levels and using suitable mechanical cutters to retain the existing shape and height. Remove any cuttings lodged in the surface of the hedge and rake up and remove all arisings.

Allow for the operation to be carried out to suit the species and position of the hedge, e.g.

Formal privet or cotoneaster hedge – once every four weeks in the main growing season (4 cuts per year).
Hawthorn boundary edge – once a year in the autumn or winter but with an additional cut in early June where it overhangs a footpath.
Beech or hornbeam hedge – once a year in late summer.

Guide times using motorized hedge trimmers:

For hedges under 1.7 m high: 1–2 hours per 100 m^2 of surface area.
For hedges over 1.7 m high: 1.5–3 hours per 100 m^2 of surface area.

Using a tractor-mounted hedge trimmer: 0.3–0.5 hours per 100 m^2 of surface area.

(b) Maintain weeds or grass growth in the base of the hedge at a maximum height of 100 mm by regular mowing, strimming or hand-cutting or by the use of Simazine plus Amitrole herbicide or approved equivalent.

Allow for mowing once every six weeks in the main growing season (four times per year).

Allow for herbicide application once a year in late spring.

Mowing, with a small rotary mower, 0.05–0.1 hours per 100 m. Herbicide application with a knapsack sprayer, 0.2–0.3 hours per 100 m.

Care of Newly Planted Trees – General

During the first few years after planting, young trees need regular attention if they are to survive and then grow. This aftercare can cost as much as 25 per cent or more of the original cost of the plant and the planting, but the extra expense is more than justified by the lower failure rate and the more rapid growth and therefore impact on the landscape.

Two important techniques have developed in recent years. The use of transparent 'tree shelters' to improve the growth rate and protect the plant against rabbits, etc. and the use of short, rather than long, stakes to encourage earlier and more stable root formation.

The most important operation of all is to keep the soil around the tree free from weeds or grass which will compete for moisture in the soil.

Maintenance objective

Establish a stable and healthily growing tree within three years from planting with a well-shaped framework for future growth.

Maintenance operations

(a) Maintain a 1-metre diameter circle of plant-free soil around the base of the tree by hoeing *or* the use of Propyzamide, Dichlobenil or other approved herbicide.

Allow for hoeing up to once every four weeks in the growing season (five times per year) (1–2 hours per 100 trees). Allow for herbicide treatment once in the winter or spring (0.3–0.5 hours per 100 trees).

Note: This operation can be replaced by the application of a mulch or black plastic ground cover.

(b)   Hand hook or otherwise cut back any tall vegetation that is threatening to shade or smother the young tree (i.e. tall vegetation growing from outside the 1-metre weed-free area).

Allow for cutting back once a year in June (0.5–1 hour per 100 trees).

(c)   Water the newly planted trees throughout the summer months (May to August) at fortnightly intervals after any period of four weeks without significant rainfall (less than 5 mm). Apply sufficient water to thoroughly wet the top 150 mm of soil around the tree roots. This will normally require approximately 10 litres for a seedling or whip and 20 litres for a standard tree. (0.5–1 hour per 100 transplanted shrubs; 1–1.5 hours per 100 standard trees, excluding transport of water to the site).

Note: The need for this operation will depend on the weather and also in the value and importance of the planting. Many plantations will survive without watering but the growth will be very limited and often be linked with shoot die-back.

Watering is much more important on very light soils or for trees planted late in the season.

(d)   Check stakes and ties for firmness and support and adjust as necessary. Allow for checking once a year, preferably in late spring (1–2 hours per 100 trees).

(e)   Firm the soil around the roots to ensure that the plant is securely planted in the ground and upright. Allow for firming once in the spring after planting (1–1.5 hours per 100 trees).

(f)   Formative prune the tree to remove any dead, diseased or damaged shoots and create a balanced form for future growth.

Allow for pruning once in the second or third year after planting (1.5–2 hours per 100 trees, extra time will be required for tall standards).

Regular Maintenance of Paved Areas – General

Although these areas are generally thought to be maintenance-free, most roadways, car parks, footpaths and paved areas need regular sweeping and weed control. In addition, drainage gulleys need emptying, an operation that is often forgotten until there is a flood.

Maintenance objective

Regularly sweep or clean the roadway/paved surface to keep it clear of litter or other debris that will detract from the appearance of the site. Keep the surface substantially free from weed growth and all drainage gulleys in working order.

Maintenance operations

(a) Sweep all paved areas at regular intervals and remove all arisings from the site. Frequency to vary according to the nature of the site. For example:

  - car parks and entrance roads – once a month
  - playgrounds or hard tennis courts – once in 1 to 3 months
  - paved quadrangles – up to once a week.

  Hand-sweeping 0.2–0.3 hours per 100 m^2
  Mechanical-sweeping 0.05–0.1 hours per 100 m^2.

(b) Control all annual weed growth by the application of Simazine plus Amitrole weedkiller, or approved equivalent. A single application in March/April should normally be sufficient but follow-up treatment may be necessary in late summer (0.2–0.5 hours per 100 m^2).

(c) Clear silt and extraneous matter from the drainage gulleys, including the lifting and replacement of the drain cover. Programme for once every six months but more frequently where silting up is a particular problem (0.1–0.2 hours per gulley).

(d) Inspect and clear any leaves and other litter from drain gulley covers. Programme at up to once a week in the autumn when and where there is likely to be heavy leaf fall (0.05–0.1 hours per gulley).

Litter Clearance – General

The presence of foreign material, as distinct from natural litter (leaves, grass cuttings, etc.), can seriously despoil any area of landscape. Various measures can be taken to try and discourage litter dumping, from on-the-spot fines to gentle persuasion, and the strategic placement of litter bins. None the less there is a need regularly to clear and tidy most sites in public use. The frequency with which this needs to be done will vary enormously from place to place and the season of the year. Planted borders in a busy shopping precinct may need clearing every day and, at the other extreme, the shrub borders around an old people's home are only likely to need litter clearance once a year, usually along with the autumn cultivations or pruning.

Deliberate fly tipping of builders' rubble, old furniture and household fittings usually requires different clearance arrangements and for that reason tends to be separated from the routine litter clearance in contract documents.

Maintenance objective

Collect and remove from the site all extraneous litter and rubbish on a regular basis so that its presence is not detrimental to the appearance of the site. (This does not mean that the site has to be free from litter all the time, but that the litter is kept to a reasonable minimum.)

Maintenance operations

(a)   Collect and remove to the contractor's tip all extraneous rubbish, not arising from maintenance works, which is detrimental to the appearance of the site. This rubbish to include stones, bricks, debris, paper, confectionery and other wrappings, bottles, cans and plastic containers.

Allow for this operation to be carried out at regular intervals based on previous experience of the site. Times need to be assessed on past experience of the site but up to 0.1 hour per 100/m^2, or more where there are special litter problems.

(b)   Collect and remove to the contractor's tip all extraneous matter which has deliberately been deposited on the site by persons known or unknown (fly-tipping). Such matter to include bricks, rubble, garden and household refuse, discarded domestic appliances, furniture and scrap metal. Priced per occasion based on an estimate of the volume of material to be collected.

Note

1. All winter games pitches will normally require spring harrowing and reseeding (up to 8 hours according to methods).

References

Bradshaw, A. D., Goode, D. A. and Thorpe, E. (eds) (1983), *Ecology and Design in Landscape*, 24th Symposium of the British Ecological Society, Manchester, Blackwell Scientific Publications

Duffey, E., Morris, M. G., Sheail, J., Ward, Lena K., Wells, D. A. and Wells T. C. E. (1974), *Grassland Ecology and Wildlife Management*, Chapman and Hall

Hanson, A. A. and Juska, F. V. (eds), *Turfgrass Science*, American Society of Agronomy, Agronomy No. 14

Way, J. M. (ed.) *Management of Vegetation*, British Crop Protection Council, Monograph No. 26

Appendix 2.I   *Average Seasonal Work-hours for Routine Maintenance*

Feature or operation	Unit	Average standard work hours per week			
		January to March	April to June	July to September	October to December
1. Cylinder lawn mowing					
a. 24″ machine. Cuttings boxed off (24 cuts per year)	100 m^2	0.02	0.12	0.11	0.07*
b. Triple ride on mower (24 cuts per year)	100 m^2	0.005	0.05	0.03	0.03*
2. Rotary lawn mowing. 18″ machine (15 cuts per year)	100 m^2	Nil	0.13	0.10	0.01
3. Shrub borders (established)	100 m^2	0.01	Nil	0.08	0.14
4. Rose borders	100 m^2	0.27	0.09	0.41	0.44
5. Herbaceous borders	100 m^2	0.13	0.95	0.89	0.31
6. Annual bedding (winter and summer)	100 m^2	0.15	1.3	0.41	1.0

*Including autumn leaf sweeping.

Chapter 3

ARRANGING THE WORKS BY CONTRACT

Modern grounds maintenance has developed over the last 100 years or so from the traditions of the large country gardens and parks of the aristocracy, and their many imitators in the aspiring middle classes. In those establishments the head gardeners and their various assistants were usually part of the household staff and, as tradition has it, relatively highly placed in the pecking order of those 'below stairs'. The employment of a head gardener and assistants was largely followed by the emerging parks departments in the late nineteenth and early twentieth centuries, and so, up until very recent times, the majority of public and private open spaces have been maintained by directly employed staff.

The direct employment of parks and garden staff has a number of advantages including:

- a reinforcement of the sense of loyalty of the staff to their employer and the sites
- continuity and the involvement of the staff in the longer-term husbandry of the sites
- good opportunities for job satisfaction and motivation easier and more direct control by the employer.

However, in many situations, the use of contractors can be equally advantageous, with particular benefits being:

- greater resources available to the employer, particularly of specialist equipment or skills

- the employer is freed from the burdens of administration and supervision and any long-term obligations to staff
- the employer does not have to provide capital for machinery and equipment
- the possibility of much more cost-effective maintenance of small sites that would not justify the employment of full-time staff.
- the potential for competition in terms of quality and price (the basis for the government's compulsory competition legislation – Local Government Act 1988).

In principle, there are no fundamental reasons why the use of direct staff or contractors should involve any differences in overall costs. On small sites, or for work requiring very special skills, it is likely that contracting will be the easiest and least expensive arrangement. However, if the work is of the scale of, say, a parks department in a large town, it is very unlikely that there would be cost or other advantages in using contractors, on the important assumption that the management and motivation of the staff is good in either alternative. The decision, therefore, for the large organization should rest on the relative merits of the alternatives, as outlined above, but include the options of using hybrid arrangements of directly employed staff being 'topped up' by specialist contractors, e.g. for work such as tree surgery, weed spraying or verge mowing. Thus, in this option, the employer would be the overall organizer of a federation of small contractors and 'in house' staff, an arrangement that gives great reserves of resources and therefore flexibility to meet unforeseen circumstances.

The assumption that the quality of management and organization is the same for contractors or direct staff organization is, of course, a critical one and, in practice, there are likely to be very large differences, with inefficient and efficient equally distributed in both the commercial and 'in house' sectors. This being the case, one of the fundamental advantages of a contract system is that it can provide the basis for valid comparisons of overall effectiveness. These comparisons are particularly important for public authorities where cost-effectiveness has to be demonstrated, as well as achieved, and it is becoming increasingly common to test the efficiency of public services by inviting competitive tenders for a closely specified level of service.

At the time of writing (Autumn 1988), this competition in the provision of grounds maintenance services is becoming a legal requirement for local authorities (Local Government Act 1988). Some detail of the legislation (under Regulations) have still to be published and implemented, but the main thrust of it is to require local authorities to:

(a) Only carry out grounds maintenance by directly employed staff if that work has been submitted to competitive tender with tenders invited from private contractors

(b) Award the contracts on the basis of lowest price

(c) Only award the contracts to 'in house' staff where such staff are formed into a financially separate 'in house' contractor

(d) Require any 'in house' contractors to operate without subsidy, bearing all relevant overhead costs and to achieve a prescribed return (5 per cent) on the capital employed

(e) Prepare the contract conditions and specifications, and invite tenders, in such a way that there is free and equal competition between 'in house' and external contractors.

These requirements will have profound effects on the way in which day-to-day grounds maintenance is organized within local authorities, where, for the most part, the work has largely been carried out by directly employed staff. In particular, it will affect the security and conditions of employment of the groundsmen and gardeners and, in turn, their motivation and attitudes to work.

In addition, there will be changes at the managerial level (see Chapter 9) and the local authorities will have to be rather more precise in setting their grounds maintenance requirements in a specification that can be used as a basis for competitive tenders. Not only will these tenders have to be explicit enough for the tenderers to price with reasonable confidence, but they will also have to be sufficiently precise for subsequent supervision of the contracts. (See Chapter 2 for sample specification clauses.)

Management of Competition

Although it is not always apparent, competition is very much part of our daily lives and, for instance, we regularly expect to compare prices when making major, or even day-to-day, purchases. In addition, competition gives us choice in the style and quality of many of the things that contribute to our lives, from the thrills of competitive sport, to means of transport, clothes, food and many other services. Gardeners know that competition helps the processes of plant selection but also has to be managed. For example, sowing seeds too thickly produces intense competition and a crop of weak and etiolated seedlings. Eliminate the competition by sowing too thinly and a different sort of competition, the weeds, need extra control.

In human affairs competition that is unlimited can lead to sweatshops, dangerous working methods, or even the race between nations to build the biggest bomb. Local authorities are now being required to use competition to help to achieve efficient services and they too need to consider how they should manage or even regulate that competition so that it really does work for the benefit of the public. These considerations can often become clouded by political dogma but the particular factors that are concerned with the technology of competition are the length and size of the contract, the form and type of the specification and the selection of the potential contractors.

Length of Contracts

Grounds maintenance is, almost by definition, an ongoing and therefore continuous process and this continuity is often critical in achieving good results. Many of the individual tasks, preparing cricket squares or establishing bedding plants, need detailed judgement and experience of the particular site that can only be developed over a number of years. In addition many of the end-

results such as well-balanced flowering shrubs or a free-flowering meadow sward, can only be achieved by consistent care and
attention over several seasons.

This requirement for continuity conflicts with the needs of
competition which must contain at least the chance of regular
changes in staff and organization. Thus, while a ten-year
contract debars any competition for many years, a one-year
contract is very unlikely to encourage the good long-term
development of the sites. Also, very short-term contracts will
not allow the contractor time to recoup the costs of employing
and training new staff or sufficient time to offset the capital
costs of machinery and transport. As a result, the costs will be
artificially high and/or the work standards be too low through
employing temporary, unskilled and uncommitted staff.

As a compromise, contracts of approximately five years are
likely to achieve satisfactory results. However, as this timespan
involves a risk to the employer of mediocre results for rather a
long time, some contracts are let on a three-year term with the
option of an extension for a further two years if the work is
satisfactory. This arrangement is particularly important when a
new or untried contractor is being employed.

Contracts of more than 12 months usually need to have
provision for updating the prices to cope with wage and other
price inflations. To do without such an arrangement would
involve the contractor in extremely speculative judgements
about the future levels of costs and such guesses are unlikely to
be in the long-term interests of either party. It is therefore usual
to hold prices firm for the first 12 months and then update
them on the basis of an agreed index, preferably at yearly
intervals to reduce administrative costs. The most appropriate
index is probably the Grounds Maintenance index GM81,
published by the Property Services Agency of the Department
of the Environment.

Size of Contract

Grounds maintenance is an essentially local activity, where the
effectiveness depends very much on the skill and judgement of

the individual operative. Economies of scale will accrue in large-scale operations through the use of specialist and high-capacity equipment and some division of labour between the skilled and simple tasks. However, these potential economies can soon be offset by the costs of transporting equipment and staff regularly from site to site, not just on a few occasions, as might be the case in a construction contract, but regularly and frequently over a long period of time.

Because of the need for frequent attendance on site, the major economies of scale are most likely to be achieved by good matching of machinery and staff to the workload and having both staff and machinery that are based as close as possible to the site or sites (see Chapter 4). For a large park or garden this will mean basing the staff, and machinery for the routine operations, actually on the site. Similarly a mobile team is best based close to the logical 'centre of gravity' of the work.

These local arrangements usually only involve a working team of two or three people and provided they are skilled and generally able to work under their own initiative, there are few economies of scale to be gained from linking them with a larger group. None the less, some savings may arise from the possibility of sharing, rather than hiring, specialist items of equipment, particularly for items like gang-mowers or 'ride-on' triple mowers that are more economic when used to their full capacity.

In practice, the most cost-effective size of a maintenance unit will depend on the exact nature of work and, for instance, a unit maintaining town centre verges and buildings surrounds will have relatively little need for gang-mowers or tractor equipment in general. However, in a school grounds maintenance service the normal independent, and cost effective, unit might consist of two mobile teams, of two or three people each, plus a gang-mower/tractor driver, i.e. 5–7 staff in all.

This unit could be a completely self-contained and efficient unit with one member being a working manager and dealing with the necessary administration and 'external' affairs. In this respect it would be similar to many agricultural or commercial horticulture units where the close and detailed attention of an owner-manager achieves very high labour utilization, and therefore good control over the major costs. This detailed supervision tends to be much less effective in larger and geographically dispersed organizations but there can be greater specialization on management of the overall enterprise and more sophisticated estimating and cost control systems. Also, the larger organization can afford to develop staff training schemes and be innovative in working techniques and experimenting with new types of machinery. All these desirable extras are, however, overheads to the main activity of providing the direct service to individual customers and therefore the unit costs are not likely to be greatly different from those of the small local firm that is well managed. This is borne out by the present structure of the industry where there is a combination of large parks departments, and a few large contractors working alongside, and in competition with, many smaller contractors.

A local authority that is contracting out its grounds maintenance can either package the work into very large parcels and benefit from any economies of scale of the large firm or in house contractor, or divide the work into much smaller parts to promote a healthy competition among a number of small businesses. As discussed above, and from the present structure of the industry, it seems likely that the overall unit costs are not likely to be greatly different but the effect on the workings of the competition will be rather more significant.

As an example, a large district council may have an annual requirement for grounds maintenance work that is equivalent to employing around 70 staff (approximately £1 million in 1988 prices). If all this work were let on a single five-year contract, the contractor should be able to achieve good economies of scale in management and use of specialist equipment. However, there would be no opportunity of testing the market again for another five years and by that time relatively few, if any, other firms are likely to be in a position to submit a competitive bid. Apart from the effective, or near, monopoly, the employer has put all his 'eggs in one basket', and will have relatively little choice if the level of service is unsatisfactory.

As an alternative, the district council could let part, or all, of the work in units equivalent to about 5–7 staff (approximately

£100,000). This would give a maximum of 10 units and, if each was let for five years, two units could be submitted for tender every year. If the economies of scale were significant for a larger organization, it would gradually be able to win additional units each, but competition should still exist as a small firm would always have the opportunity of winning back at least some of the work. For the employer, this arrangement would give the benefits of effective competition at reasonable unit costs, and limit the undesirable consequences of a mediocre or unsatisfactory contractor. Furthermore, the gradual contraction or expansion of one organization against another, over a five-year period, is likely to give greater stability for the employees, the grounds staff and gardeners, and security of employment over a longer period.

Selection of Contractors

Choosing the right contractor is essential for almost any project but is even more so for something that is as long term as grounds maintenance, and is likely to involve close working relationships with the people who use the sites as well as those who administer the contract. The final selection is usually based on the price that the contractor tenders for the work in question but, if this is used as the sole criterion, there is a considerable risk of employing someone who is not sufficiently skilled, does not have the resources to supply the service consistently, or is generally unreliable.

The most common procedure is therefore first to draw up a select list of contractors and invite tenders from them once it has been established, via bankers and other references, that they are capable of coping with the type and scale of the proposed contract. The outline procedure would therefore be as follows:

1. Advertise the fact that tenders are to be sought and ask prospective contractors to apply. Outline type of work, approximate value of it, and likely length of contract. Also explain where a detailed specification can be examined. (Alternatively, specifications can be provided at a realistic fee.)
2. Ask prospective contractors to complete an application

form so that they can be considered for an approved list (see Appendix 3.I).

3. Take up references for prospective contractors and, if appropriate, visit their premises or work sites.

4. Prepare an approved list of those contractors who appear to be capable of undertaking the proposed contract.

5. Send tender documents to all those on the approved list or else a select list of a smaller number who are most likely to be suited to the particular project. (A large number of tenderers is wasteful of their time and is expensive to the employer. For most maintenance contracts between three and six tenders should be adequate.)

6. Receive, assess and check the tenders after allowing sufficient time to price the specification (usually at least three weeks but preferably six weeks).

7. Award the contract after any necessary consultation with the client. (The contract would normally be awarded on the basis of lowest price as the contractors have already been assessed as competent.)

8. Inform the unsuccessful clients of the tender prices received without identifying the winning contractor or the contractors submitting the other prices. (This lets the contractors know how they fared and how they may have to improve their prices in future and thus sharpens the competition.)

9. Hold a pre-start meeting to outline the supervision arrangements and agree any outstanding details. (The start date will normally have been included in the specification. Comprehensive maintenance contracts should usually start in the late autumn so that the contractor has time to build up his staff and machinery and get the sites into good order before the growing season.)

(See also Code for Single Stage Select Tenders published by the NJCC)

Forms of Contract for Landscape Maintenance

As relatively little landscape maintenance work has been carried out by contract the present 'state of the art' of maintenance contract is not yet very highly developed compared, for instance, with the construction and building industries. However, a number of contract forms are now being developed in preparation for the onset of compulsory competitive tendering. Among these are the Form of Contract and Specification for Grounds Maintenance, prepared by the association of Chief Technical Officers (ACTO), and one prepared by the Joint Council for Landscape Industries (JCLI). Both of these forms still need further development before they could be recommended as a standard form but they do offer a very valuable guide to the type of document that will have to be developed in the future. The ACTO documents suggest some different forms that can be used, e.g. for unit rate or lump-sum contracts, while the JCLI concentrates more on the specifications and gives some alternatives of operation or performance-based definitions (see later section of this chapter).

Whatever the detailed form the contract documents should consist of the following:

- A form of tender on which the contractor states his price. (This may be designed so that it can also act as a form of agreement when the contractor is signed)
- General conditions of contract
- Preliminaries to the specification
- The specification of the works
- A bill of quantities or a priced specification.

General Conditions of Contract

The form of tender and general conditions of contract can be based on the established documents used in landscape construction contracts, e.g. the JCLI form of contract for landscape works. However, some of the wording may need to be altered to suit the maintenance requirements and certain of the clauses, e.g. for defects liability period would be unnecessary. Suitable alterations are indicated in the JCLI recommendations for Maintenance of Grounds contract but, whatever the alterations, the general conditions should at least cover the following items:

1. The execution of the works. What is expected of the

parties to the contract. Arrangements for dealing with variations and alterations to the works and how the works will be controlled.

2. Subcontracting. The employer's policy on subcontracting. For maintenance contracts this is only likely to be allowed for specialist works.
3. The period of the contract. The starting and finishing time during which the contractor will be required to maintain the sites.
4. Payments. According to the work completed or prefixed payments based on a satisfactory standard of maintenance (see later section). Arrangements for alterations and extras. Arrangements for dealing with fluctuating cost or updating fixed price contracts for annual inflation.
5. Insurances and responsibility for injury and damage. The contractor to take out insurance policies to meet any claims arising from the carrying out of the works.
6. Terminations and disputes. Conditions under which the contract can be terminated by either party and arrangements for settling disputes, e.g. by arbitration.
7. Workpeople. Their suitability, behaviour, dress and means of identification.
8. Avoidance of noise and nuisance. To site users and neighbouring properties. Restriction on working outside 'normal' hours. Trespass is not permitted onto adjoining sites.
9. Depots and conveniences. Contractors' responsibility or provision by the employer.
10. Advertising. Employer's agreement or otherwise to erection of signboards, etc., by the contractor.

Preliminary Items

The preliminaries to the specification may at first sight appear to cover some of the items in the general conditions of contract, but they are generally matters which are more specific to the particular contract. The preliminary items are usually included at the start of the specification so that the contractor can price them separately from the main parts of the work. These prices then represent the costs to the contractor of setting up the organization necessary for the starting and other overheads of the works. Likely preliminaries for a grounds maintenance specification are:

1. Costs of complying with the general conditions of contract
2. The works to be carried out in such a way that they facilitate and do not interfere with the normal site uses, e.g. will prepare pitches for sports fixtures and will not interfere with play.
3. The access arrangements onto the sites
4. The provision of a suitable supervisor to attend meetings and/or receive instructions during normal working hours
5. Requirements for workpeople to report on site when they start work, carry identification cards and wear any uniform or special clothing
6. Special safety instructions, over and above those required by statute, e.g. on the use of herbicides on school sites or nature areas or use of machinery near to site visitors
7. Need to report vandalism or the need for extra work
8. Need to supply work records, time-sheets or other information as the work progresses
9. The disposal of litter, grass clippings, prunings, etc. and approvals for composting or burning on site
10. Any costs of establishing working bases or special depots prior to carrying out the contract.

Specifications Clauses

Whatever the form or conditions of contract, the contract specification is of fundamental importance as it is the only yardstick for assessing the work that is required. The specification must therefore be clear enough to give an adequate description of the work and anything that might influence its completion, and be precise enough to act as a reasonable basis for settling any disputes that might arise.

The specification clauses can be arranged in a number of different ways depending on the scope of the works. The following list includes the items most likely to be needed.

Lawns, verges and other grass areas
Rose, shrub and groundcover borders
Herbaceous borders
Seasonal bedding areas
Fence lines and hedges
Trees
Upkeep of hard surfaces
Sweeping and clearance of litter
Mowing and general maintenance of grass playing fields
Special maintenance of grass sports pitches; football, rugby, cricket, tennis, athletics, etc.
Upkeep of jumping pits and care of sports equipment
Upkeep of synthetic or hard porous pitches.

(Sample clauses under these various headings are included in Chapter 2.)

Depending on the range of tasks in the contract, the specification clauses can be framed to concentrate on either the details of the tasks (operations specification) or the result that is to be achieved (performance specification). Thus in stark contrast the mowing of a lawn could be specified as:

(a) Mow with a specified mower, set at a certain height, when directed by the employer or at set intervals. Or,

(b) Mow as necessary to keep the grass growth neatly trimmed between certain heights.

In the first instance the contractor has to do exactly what he is told (and is paid for exactly what is done). He is hired, in the main, for his muscle and machinery and will receive more or less money, throughout the season, depending on the weather and the employer's decisions.

Under the second arrangement the contractor has to exercise some skill and judgement, as well as physical ability, in deciding when and how to keep the lawn looking like a lawn. The employer will probably pay a fixed lump-sum to cover the cost throughout the season and the risks and benefits of bad or good weather will tend to be shared between both parties to the contract.

In most circumstances, it is likely that the performance-based specification will give the greatest opportunity for skilled staff to excel and maintain a pride and interest in the work and sites. Overall quality (as compared with the completion of specific operations) is likely to be better, the employer is freed from the detailed day-to-day management of the work and administration of the contract (supervision, checking of invoices, etc.) can be kept to the minimum.

For some types of work the employer may well wish to keep rather greater control over the detailed operations and, therefore, use an operation-based specification or a series of unit rates that can be ordered as and when necessary, e.g. for the mowing of road verges, weed control in woodland plantations or the management of nature conservation sites or wildflower meadows.

The distinction between performance and operation-based specifications is not clear-cut, and the terms therefore apply to an approach to specification writing rather than separate descriptions of the work. In a comprehensive maintenance specification, some items may be defined in terms of performance, e.g. grass mowing to within certain heights, and others by means of the operations, e.g. cut the hedge in June. A slavish adherence to one form or the other is unlikely to be helpful and the important end-result is that the contractor understands exactly what he is asked to price and what flexibility he is likely to have in carrying out the work, and so achieve the specified end result.

Bill of Quantities and Schedule of Rates

A bill of quantities giving the measured areas or lengths of the work is essential for all but the smallest job. It can either be kept as a separate section of the tender or combined with the specification. Keeping the quantities separate is convenient for the comparison of the prices and cost-control purposes, particularly if the specification clauses are long and complex. However, combining the specification and quantities can make it easier to price and gives a more direct and easy reference between the cost and the exact work required.

It is of considerable advantage also to ask the contractors to quote prices for a schedule of day and unit rates which can be used for agreeing the charges for additions or reductions to the specification. An example is given in Figure 3.1.

Payment Systems

The charges to the client, or valuation of the work, can be arranged in a number of different ways but there are three main systems of measurement and valuation that are suitable for competitive tenders for grounds maintenance. These are:

1. Based on a schedule of rates. The schedule consists of a series of work specifications which the tenderer is asked to price for a unit of measurement, e.g. square metre of grass or lengths of edging. No precise quantities are given but estimated amounts are shown to give the likely volume of work.

    The client may sometimes insert the rates for the work and ask the tenderers to indicate their percentage increase or decrease on this price.

    The client will order the work on the lowest-priced contract or as and when the work is required up to 'saturation' point when that contractor cannot undertake any more. Work will then be ordered on the next lowest-priced contractor. This arrangement is usually only suitable, in grounds maintenance, for intermittent or irregular work.

2. Lump-sum contract based on specifications and bills of quantities. In this form the quantities of work are included and so the contractor quotes the rate for each item of work and by multiplication and addition, the total lump-sum for the work.

    Alterations and additions to the work can easily be

All rates to include transport to the sites in the contract area, provision of staff, supervision, fuel and other materials.

1. Day or hourly rates	£ rate per day	£ rate per hour
a. Gardener with hand tools		
b. Gardener with small rotary or cylinder mower (up to 500 mm wide)		
c. Gardener with hedge trimmer, chainsaw or strimmer		
d. Gardener with knapsack sprayer to apply residual herbicide		
e. Tractor with mounted or trailed cultivators or rollers		
f. Tractor with 5-unit trailed gang-mower		
g. Tractor with side mounted flail mower (1.5 m cut)		

2. Unit rates	£ rate per 100 m^2	£ rate per hectare
a. Tractor gang mowing (5 unit)		
b. 'Triple' cylinder mowing		
c. Rotary mowing pedestrian machine		
d. Hedge trimming excluding clearing of clippings		
(i) Hedge below 1.5 m		
(ii) Hedge up to 3 m		
e. Supply and spread playing field fertilizer		
(i) autumn		
5:10:10 @ 300 kg/hectare		
(ii) spring		
15:10:10 @ 450 kg/hectare		

Figure 3.1   *Schedule of day and unit rates*

made and a new price agreed according to the rates quoted. This is an ideal arrangement where the volume and content of the work will be varied throughout the year with, for instance, grass mowing being as and when instructed by the client.

3.   Lump-sum based on specification. In this form the quantities of work are given for guidance but the contrac-

Month	Proportion of contract sum	Month	Proportion of contract sum
January	$\frac{1}{24}$ per month	July	$\frac{3}{24}$ per month
February	$\frac{1}{24}$ per month	August	$\frac{3}{24}$ per month
March	$\frac{1}{24}$ per month	September	$\frac{3}{24}$ per month
April	$\frac{3}{24}$ per month	October	$\frac{1}{24}$ per month
May	$\frac{3}{24}$ per month	November	$\frac{1}{24}$ per month
June	$\frac{3}{24}$ per month	December	$\frac{1}{24}$ per month

Figure 3.2 *Monthly payments of an annual lump-sum contract*

tor gives tender prices for the whole of the work rather than according to the measured quantities. This arrangement is suitable when the contractor, as in a performance specification, is expected to achieve a certain standard throughout the whole year. Some unit rates can be included as a basis for variations but these rates, as they will only apply to variations, will not necessarily relate to the overall lump-sums.

Whatever system is adopted for valuation and measurement it is normal for the contractor to be paid on a monthly basis in response to the submission of an invoice. Where the work is ordered item by item by the employer, as in (1) above, the invoice will be based on the work actually completed. However, in the case of longer-term arrangements, the contractor is more likely to be paid in monthly instalments of the total annual sum (plus or minus any variations). These monthly instalments should preferably match the seasonal variation in workload as for example in Figure 3.2.

Quality Control

Throughout the period of the contract, arrangements must be made to check that the contractor is carrying out the work according to the specification. The frequency and intensity of those checks or inspections will vary according to the way in which the work is ordered and the reliability or otherwise of the contractor. Thus, if the work is ordered item by item then each item will need to be inspected as it is completed and probably this might involve at least weekly site inspections. Under a lump-sum contract, with a reliable contractor, the frequency can be much reduced, or even be based on a spot-check of sample areas.

Where inspections reveal failure on the part of the contractor to carry out the work on time or to the specification, the following procedure, or one similar to it, should be adopted.

(a)   The contractor be instructed to put right or complete the work within a reasonable time.

(b)   All payments suspended (other than those already certified) until all the work is completed or put right.

(c)   Once the work is completed or put right, the monthly payment is reduced by the value of that item that was below standard during that month.

(d)   If the contractor fails to put the work right, the employer will normally have the right, under the general conditions of the contract either to determine the contract or employ others to do the work and deduct the extra cost of doing so from monies owing to the contractor.

(e)   If the contractor puts the work right when directed but is still generally unreliable, the employer may, subject to the conditions of contract, determine the contract after a certain number of failures have been notified, e.g. 15 failures in any three month period.

Actions under (d) and (e) should only occur in extreme cases but the contract conditions and methods of payments should be designed to protect the employer from additional costs or financial losses in such circumstances. In landscape construction contracts it is usual to quote liquidated and ascertained damages that will be payable in the event of the work not being completed on time. This procedure is not likely to be appropriate in maintenance contracts and of relatively little value where the practical need is to get the work completed as quickly as possible. In most circumstances, therefore, the reduced or delayed payments, as set out above, are likely to give sufficient incentive to the contractor. In addition, as the contractor is paid at least one month in arrears, the employer will usually have sufficient money in hand to meet the extra costs of determining the contract and if necessary, having the work done by others.

As a supplement to the above, the employer may ask the contractor to take out a financial bond, with a reputable bank or insurance company, that will indemnify the employer against any costs resulting from the failure of the contractor to carry out the work. Such a bond is highly desirable in a very large contract where the contractor would be difficult to replace, but is of much less value for medium to small contracts, of say less than £250,000 per annum.

In carrying out grounds maintenance under a contract, the financial controls should really only be regarded as a backup in the event of serious failure. The main security of a regular and satisfactory grounds maintenance service rests in only employing reliable and competent contractors and being vigilant in quality control so that any faults are quickly noted and brought to the attention of the contractor. For these purposes it is essential to employ a competent landscape Clerk of Works who has experience of grounds maintenance and the charges for this must be taken into account when estimating the annual costs of the work. The volume of work that can be effectively supervised by a single full-time Clerk of Works can only effectively be assessed in the light of experience but as a general guide it is likely to be of the order of £300–500,000 in 1988 prices (i.e. up to 5 per cent on cost, including overheads).

Appendix 3.I

Application for Inclusion on the Approved List of Contractors for Landscape Construction and Maintenance Works.

1. *General details*

Name of company or organisation

State whether registered company, partnership or sole trader

Name of director or manager and address for correspondence purposes only	Address of registered office (if applicable)
Post code Telephone no.	
VAT reg. no.	Company reg. no.

Construction Industry Tax Deduction Scheme		
Certificate no.	Certificate type (714, I,P or C)	Expiry date

2. *Public liability insurance*

Underwriter	Name and address of broker
	Post code Telephone no.
Date policy falls due for renewal	

The Council requires a minimum level of cover of £1,000,000 in respect of any one incident together with an indemnity to principals clause and cover in respect of the use of subcontractors. A copy of your policy in force at the time will be required as a condition of contract for any work you undertake for the county council.

3. *Scope and structure of your organisation*

Please provide information in respect of the following:

(a) The type of work for which you wish to be considered and state the minimum and maximum financial limits.

	Financial limits	
	Min.	Max.
General landscaping works including planting	....	....
Playing field construction	....	....
Grounds maintenance including the upkeep of sports pitches	....	....
Others (specify)	....	....

(b) The areas of the county in which you are prepared to work.

(c) The number of staff directly employed by your Organisation during the last year as:

Number

(i)   landscape manual workers
(ii)   working foremen/chargehands
(iii)   supervisors/managers
(iv)   office/administration staff

(d) The proportion of your financial turnover in the last financial year which was accounted for by subcontractors (including labour only contracts).

Percentage ....

(e) The vehicles, plant and machinery you have at your disposal, i.e. wholly owned by you or under lease, and its age.

Description   Number   Average age

Please continue on a separate sheet if necessary.

(f) Training and safety policies. Please attach a copy of your safety and training policy, and make here any particular statements on the safety of the General Public and of the site users.

4. *Employer references*

Please give the names and addresses of three public bodies or companies (preferably including at least one local authority) to whom I may write for references and for whom you have worked during the last two years.

	Name	Address
1		
2		
3		

5. *Financial information*

(a) State your trading turnover for the last financial year.

£ ....

(b) State the total value of any loans or debts for which you are currently liable as a trading organisation.

£ ....
Note:
In the case of public limited companies please attach a copy of your audited accounts for the last financial year.

(c) Please give the name and address of your banker from whom confidential financial references may be obtained.

6. *General supporting statement in respect of this application:*

Signed .... Date ....

Position ....

References

Department of the Environment Property Services Agency,
Updating Percentage Adjustments for Measured Term Contracts.
Copies obtainable from
    Property Services Agency Library,
    Sales Office
    Room COO5
    Whitgift Centre
    Croydon CR9 3LY

Code of Procedure for Single Stage Selective Tendering, published
for the National Joint Consultative Committee for Building by
    RIBA Publications Limited
    66 Portland Place
    London W1N 4AD

*Grounds Maintenance. Model Form of Tender and Contract Docu-
ments (January 1987)*, prepared by the Joint Council for Landscape Industries and published by the
    British Association of Landscape Industries .
    Landscape House
    Keighley
    West Yorkshire BD21 3DR

Contract for Grounds Maintenance Forms PW2, PW4, PW2T and
PW4T, 1st edition 1987, published by
    Association of Chief Technical Officers
    Booth Street
    Nelson
    Lancashire

Chapter 4

STAFFING LEVELS AND WORKING HOURS

Seasonal Factors

Grounds maintenance is an inherently seasonal activity with frantic 'harvest' periods in the summer months and more relaxed seasons when the work can be pursued with less urgency. The seasonal variation in workload depends on the nature and layout of the sites and, in general terms, the more varied the features, the greater the continuity of work throughout the year. At one extreme is the large estate garden with vegetable plots, heated greenhouses and elaborate summer bedding and herbaceous borders. This will almost certainly require a permanent workforce, fully employed, throughout the whole year. At the other extreme, the care of housing estate road verges, without any street trees, is only likely to require regular mowing for up to 30 weeks of the year and no routine care through the winter months. A more common example is shown in Figure 4.1.

To some extent the winter shortfall of routine work is offset by a variety of 'one-off' tasks that provide some extra employment, e.g. refurbishment or replanting of shrub borders. Even these extras are unlikely completely to fill the gaps sufficiently to justify employing full-time permanent staff and the manager needs to develop various staffing and other strategies to overcome the basic problem. In essence these are shown in Figure

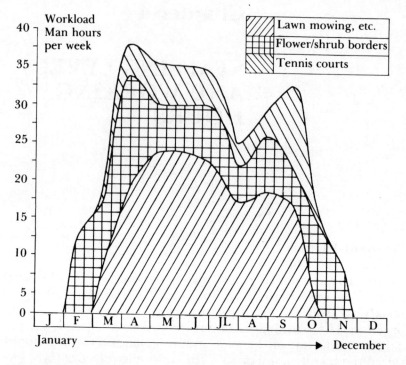

Figure 4.1   *Seasonal work pattern of routine grounds maintenance (office complex with grass tennis courts)*

4.2 and are:

- seasonal working hours/overtime or staffing (see later section)
- mechanization of peak tasks
- 'Work-spreading' techniques
- diversification of activities

Mechanization, particularly of grass mowing, will help to reduce the manpower requirements in early spring and summer, and this will justify using capital-expensive machines, even though they may not be fully utilised. Conversely, intensive mechanization of 'off-peak' tasks, e.g. winter cultivations or leaf sweeping, is less likely to bring overall savings unless alternative work is required from labour time that is saved.

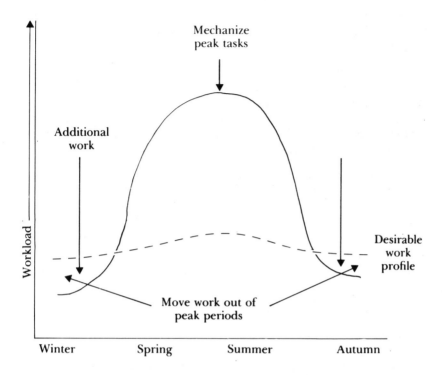

Figure 4.2 *Strategies to even out seasonal workloads*

Work-spreading techniques can be simply delaying some tasks until a quieter season, e.g. some hedge-cutting or pruning, or using maintenance regimes that take work out of the peak periods. The use of residual herbicides not only saves labour in comparison with hand hoeing but also moves the tasks to an easier time of year (early spring). As another example, the adoption of some meadow culture techniques (see Chapter 2) avoids the need for early summer mowing when most formal swards are growing at a maximum. Similar savings can be made by spraying growth retardants onto formal swards, at relatively low concentrations so that the growth is delayed for a few weeks until the peak growing season has passed.

Diversification of activities usually means taking on other grounds-related tasks during the winter months. Some landscape construction, turfing, etc. is possible, but this may often be limited by the soil conditions. Other tasks are less limited and might include:

- new planting works
- forestry and tree surgery operations
- fencing repairs or installation
- hard landscaping, new paving, etc., or repairs
- overhaul and repairs to machinery, sports equipment, etc.
- building repairs and maintenance.

Many of these tasks require quite different skills from the routine grounds maintenance and not many grounds staff will necessarily be able to achieve the same working rates, or sometimes quality of finish, that would be expected from full-time professionals. None the less, with adequate training and experience, very good results can be achieved at an economic cost to the employer and increase the job satisfaction of the staff.

Calculation of Workloads

Many experienced managers will be able to estimate, almost by eye, the likely staffing levels that are likely to be needed to keep a particular site to a given standard. However, these estimates are unlikely to be adequate for detailed contract pricing or provide accurate enough information for assessing workloads on a group of different sites, particularly if the staff are in dispute about what they should be achieving. It is therefore necessary to measure or have information on the following:

- the standard of upkeep that is to be achieved, i.e. the frequency of the main operations
- the areas/lengths of work involved
- the average time, per unit area, that is required for the tasks.

The frequency of operations and quantities of work may be available from a maintenance plan or will need to be measured as set out in Chapter 1. The times for the tasks can ideally be obtained from work study measurements (see Chapter 5) or from less sophisticated estimates. Whatever method is used however, it is essential that the work-times are understood and accepted by the staff concerned.

In most circumstances the prime need will be to assess the peak workload. At the extreme this peak might occur in one particular week of the year but, in practice, the timing of many tasks can be moved to spread the peaks over a number of weeks (even if overtime has to be worked to cope with bad weather, breakdowns or other contingencies). It is therefore sensible to average the workload over a 4–6 week period. In the example shown in Table 4.1, a six-week period has been used so that a single period will include at least one cut of the informal grass areas.

Calculation of Labour Needs

The figures from this calculation in Table 4.1 give a measure of the standard labour-hours that are likely to be required throughout each season of the year to carry out the routine maintenance on the particular site. This site is likely to be one of a number to be maintained and adding the figures together from all the sites will give the standard hours of work required, for instance, from a mobile team.

In calculating how many sites the team can be expected to look after, or how many staff are needed in the team, it is necessary to take account of:

- the likely rate of working of the staff (above or below the standard times)
- the number of productive work hours the staff are likely to achieve in the average week.

Rates of working of performance are discussed in more detail in Chapter 5 under work study. However standard times are averages and individuals or specific teams are bound to vary from the average for a number of reasons. These could be the levels of experience, poor or good motivation, good or bad organization, good or bad equipment, etc. As a result the variations can be very significant with the low achievers taking

Table 4.1 *Calculation of seasonal workload*

Operation	Area/length	Unit* time	Time per occasion	April–mid-May F	Total	Mid-May–June F	Total	July–Mid-Aug. F	Total	Mid-Aug.–Sept. F	Total
Lawns, etc.											
Mow and box off main lawns	2600 m²	·14	3·64}	5	18·60	5	18·60	4	14·88	4	14·88
Mow round obstructions	27 items	·3	·08}								
Edge clipping	315 m	·42	1·32	3	3·96	3	3·96	2	2·64	2	2·64
Recut kerb edges	75 m	·49	·37	—		—		—		1	·37
Rotary mow bulb areas	215 m²	·19	·41			1	·41	1	·41	1	·41
Spray mowing strips and fence lines	239 m	·15	·36	1	·36	—		—		—	
Rose and shrub borders											
Winter cultivation	766 m²	3·7	28·34	—		—		—		—	
Apply herbicide	766 m²	·31	2·37	—		—		—		—	
Prune shrubs	506 m²	1·0	5·06	—		—		—		—	
Prune roses	260 m²	2·8	7·28	—		—		—		—	
Dead head roses	260 m²	1·4	3·64	—		1	3·64	1	3·64	—	
Spot weed	166 m²	·15	1·15	1	1·15	2	2·30	2	2·30	1	1·15
Hedges											
Clip beech (<1·5 m)	315 m²	1·1	3·47	—		—		—		1	3·47
Clip privet (<1·5 m)	245 m²	1·1	2·70	—		1	2·70	1	2·70	1	2·70
			Sub-total		24·07		31·61		29·06		23·62
Travel and preparation times (2 staff)	—	—	·60	(5)	3·00	(5)	3·00	(4)	2·40	(4)	2·40
			Total hours		27·07		34·61		31·46		26·02
			Average per week		4·50		5·80		5·20		4·30

*Hours/100 units

Normal working hours	40 per week	
Less – Wet time	5% (assumes some wet weather working)	
– Breakdowns, etc.	5%	
– Sickness	2– 5%	
– Machinery servicing	5%	
– Training	1– 2%	
– Leave and bank		Both may be restricted
holidays	8% (or more)	in the peak seasons
Sub-total	18–30%	
Productive hours	32.8–28 per week	

Figure 4.3 *Average productive and non-productive times*

two or even three times as long as the best to arrive at the same result. Thus, if the job times used in Figure 4.2 represented carefully measured standard performance work study times and the staff were working to a well-run incentive scheme, the actual work times would probably be similar to, or slightly less than, the figures shown. Conversely, if the staff were relatively unmotivated and not working to any set programme, they would probably take up to twice the times shown.

The number of productive working hours per week or month are also likely to vary according to the motivation and organization of the team but, based on a normal 40-hour working week the losses through non-productive time could be of the order shown in Figure 4.3

The likely productive hours in Figure 4.3 may be increased by any regular overtime working, but in order to calculate the staff numbers required it is necessary to divide the total standard hours by the forecast productive hours per week.

$$\text{e.g.} \quad \frac{120 \text{ standard hours per week}}{30 \text{ productive hours per week}} \times \frac{100}{80 \text{ performance}} = 5 \text{ staff}$$

Or, if the staff were fit, healthy and well motivated,

$$\text{e.g.} \quad \frac{120 \text{ standard hours per week}}{32 \text{ productive hours per week}} \times \frac{100}{110 \text{ performance}} = 3.4 \text{ staff}$$

(or 4 staff with time for more work).

Seasonal Variations in Working Hours

Using the calculations shown above it is possible to achieve a relatively close matching of staff numbers to the expected peak workload. This in itself goes a long way towards cost-efficient staffing but, for really effective working, the annual working hours need to be distributed to meet the seasonal changes in the workload.

The normal desire of most people to have reasonably regular working hours, and pay, throughout the year can seriously conflict with the varying seasonal workload of grounds maintenance. In local authorities in particular these conflicts are potentially heightened by relatively rigid conditions of employment based on national negotiations. More flexible arrangements are therefore likely to be found in the smaller, private-sector organizations with the most flexible working arrangements of all being a one-person self-employed contractor. He, or she, will probably be able to choose the most suitable times of day to work, varying it from day to day as the weather dictates and packing up and going home, or shopping, as soon as the rain or other reasons stop work.

Such extremes, however desirable, are unlikely to be developed in normal paid employment but a number of accepted means are used, or being proposed to match working hours to the tasks in hand.

Overtime

A common and effective way of increasing the working hours to cope with sudden or peak work demands. In time of emergency staff will usually be prepared to work a great deal of overtime but over a longer period of time it is likely that most people will not want to work more than an extra 10 per cent or so of their normal hours, i.e. around 4 hours/week. Thus as a means of coping with a seasonal peak of mowing, lasting for 10–12 weeks, overtime should only be relied upon to increase the average work output by around this 10 per cent.

Overtime is usually paid at $1\frac{1}{2}$ times the normal hourly rate (and twice the rate of Sundays) but this extra premium is partially offset by the following:

- overtime allows the fixed overheads to be spread over a larger base
- all the overtime hours are working hours, i.e. there should be no losses through wet time, breakdowns or sickness
- overtime can increase the proportion of the working day that is fully productive.

This third factor is only important where there is a significant amount of daily preparation time or travelling to get to the work site. For example, if one hour of the day is spent in loading up and travelling to and from the site the unit cost per hour of work for a normal 8-hour day is 8/7 of the hourly rate. Only if the travelling, etc., accounts for around three hours per day will overtime, at time and a half, bring about a comparative reduction in the net hourly rate for productive work. For example:

(a) If the non-productive time is 1 hour per day, working 2 hours overtime increases the net rate from: $\frac{8}{7} = 1.14R$ to $\frac{11}{9} = 1.22R$ for each productive hour (an increase of 7 per cent).

(b) If the non-productive time is 3 hours per day, the 2 hours overtime will decrease the net rate from: $\frac{8}{5} = 1.6R$ to $\frac{11}{7} = 1.58R$ (A decrease of just over 1 per cent).

Where R is the basic hourly rate.

In contrast, overtime that is worked at a weekend, or on a rest day, is consistently more expensive, and the most expensive, but often a common arrangement is to work an extra half-day on Saturday mornings. Thus even if the non-productive time of preparation and travelling is only half an hour the net cost is $\frac{6}{3.5}$ or 1.71 compared with a normal 8-hour day cost of $\frac{8}{7.5}$ or 1.07 of the normal hourly rate.

'Emergency' overtime on Saturday mornings and even Sundays is often necessary to cope with bad weather or lost time during the week but it should only be used as a short-term measure, in preference to overtime as an addition to a weekday.

None the less, for certain types of heavy work it may be that the productivity will be higher during a short working morning rather than at the end of a long day, but this has to be evaluated carefully against the probable increase in net wage costs of at least 60–70 per cent.

Seasonal overtime is a much more attractive proposition as an alternative to employing full-time permanent staff. For example, the peak of summer work in a locality might require a full-time person, 40 hours a week, for around 20 weeks of the year, but there is only enough work to keep that person actively employed for an average of 10 hours a week for the rest of the year. Assuming it was possible for other staff in the area to cover the work in overtime they would probably only have to work about 35 hours extra in the summer weeks (assuming there was no extra travelling or preparation time involved). However, the extra winter work would require an exactly similar number of overtime hours. Thus the wage costs, in terms of basic, or plain time, hourly wage rates would be:

(a) For a full-time permanent member of staff
    40 hours × 52 weeks = 2080 plain time hours
(b) For equivalent overtime payments
        35 hours × 20 weeks =   700
    +10 hours × 32 weeks =   320

$$1020 \times 1.5 = 1530 \text{ plain time hours}$$

i.e. a saving of 550 plain time hours.

Although these circumstances may be fairly typical, the advantages of overtime compared with an extra worker will vary considerably according to the peakiness of the seasonal workload. In mathematical terms the overtime loses its advantage if a full-time worker could be fully employed for around 40 weeks of the year. In practice this would be a long time for the other staff to work consistent overtime but overtime, if properly managed, is a very cost-effective way of coping with an early flush of grass growth or the busy changeover period from winter to summer sports.

Temporary Staff

In theory the employment of temporary seasonal labour should be more financially attractive than overtime working and, where reliable and adequately skilled staff are available, it is an ideal arrangement. It is used extensively in commercial horticulture for fruit-picking and the like but, in recent years, good temporary staff have become more difficult to retain, particularly in areas of low unemployment.

Students can be useful temporary employees but, for most grounds maintenance work, they tend to finish their exams and college terms rather too late in the year and are therefore more useful as back-up staff during the summer holidays.

Active, retired grounds staff can be very useful as seasonal help, particularly as they may have experience and skills that are lacking in younger full-time employees.

Seasonal Working Hours

A number of employees have negotiated agreements with their staff for a seasonal variation in the working week. Typical examples based on an average 39-hour week are:

- 42 hours a week for the summer six months, and 36 hours in the winter. (A simple movement of working hours from winter to summer.)
- 40 hours a week in the summer and 37½ hours in the winter. (Based on the assumption that the extra hour in the summer is equivalent to an hour's overtime at time and a half.)

More sophisticated patterns to match the expected workload can be adopted, but staff are not likely to accept excessive hours in the summer when they themselves will want to enjoy any fine weather or tend their own gardens.

In most schemes the weekly wage remains constant throughout the year.

The advantages to an employer are that for each extra hour in the summer, the summer time or even the permanent staff level can be reduced by about 2–3 per cent and, therefore, such arrangements are often part of a productivity agreement.

Flexitime Arrangements

These are relatively commonplace for office workers but have not generally been adopted for manual workers, often because supervisors feel that the discipline of time-keeping will be more difficult to maintain. However, as productivity agreements move towards payment for a finished result, rather than completion of specific tasks, the need for strict time-keeping becomes less important.

An arrangement that allows staff to pack up and go home, when rain has obviously stopped work for the day, would be a commonsense one. However, there would need to be limits on the number of hours credit or debit that could be carried forward from week to week (probably only 2–4 hours), if only to ensure that the system was not used by the employer as a means for avoiding established premium rates for overtime.

Other Working Patterns

During the last half-century there has been a steady reduction in the average working week, the working year and even the working life. At the start these parameters could all be linked to around 49–49 hours a week, for 49 weeks a year, for 49 years. For some the 35-hour week is now a fact and it has been predicted that we may all be moving towards working lives in 35s – 35 hours for 35 weeks for 35 years.

Longer holidays for grounds staff mean that increasingly they cannot be arranged around the 'harvest' periods, and staffing levels will have to be increased accordingly.

A shorter working week will encourage the development of job-sharing arrangements, particularly on parks and golf courses that need a seven days a week presence. It may also foster shift-working arrangements on gang-mowers or other big items of equipment.

Finally, the shorter working life will probably be reflected in more full-time training in the early years, perhaps sabbatical breaks midway, and then earlier or partial retirement. Most grounds staff have to do relatively hard physical work but, in common with farm workers, they have not established the benefits of early retirement that are afforded to groups like miners, policemen and firemen. Perhaps, therefore, systems could be developed that will allow partial retirement at least to avoid the rigours of working outdoors through the worst of the winter months.

Chapter 5

STAFF ORGANIZATION AND MOTIVATION

Use of Skills and Team Working

As landscape maintenance is generally labour-intensive it is obviously very important that the staff are organized to make the best use of their time, their individual skills and aptitudes, and the machinery and equipment they use. This inevitably involves some division of labour with each man and woman having their own special skill and task, although, ideally, being able to assist or stand in for one another whenever the need arises.

This division of labour is not possible when a gardener or groundsman works entirely on his own. Thus if he is a skilled man he will be comparatively underemployed for much of his time in carrying out simple mundane tasks. Worse still, the work will be left completely undone if he falls sick or even takes a holiday. For this reason alone, it might be better to employ a contractor with adequate back-up staff and machinery, rather than relying on a gardener who works alone.

For contractors or public authorities with a large staff, there are two basic approaches to the division of labour. On the one hand, individuals can be trained to be specialist skilled operatives for a limited range of tasks which they perform almost continuously while the need arises. A gang-mower driver is a good example, although others might specialize in hedge-cutting, verge-mowing or spraying herbicides. This type of specialization makes very good use of the equipment; a single large rotary mower could be used to cut all the rough grass areas in a given geographical area. It also involves a minimum of training and the staff become specialist at operating and maintaining a particular piece of equipment. Also, they can take pride in doing it well, particularly if they would have difficulty in encompassing a wider range of tasks. The need to transport several different sets of equipment separately, from site to site, could be a disadvantage, but the general system could work very well on, say, a large park, or in a town centre where there are a number of areas to be maintained in close proximity. The disadvantages are that the staff themselves may get bored with little variation in their work and their pride and satisfaction tends to be directed towards the operation rather than the overall finished result.

The alternative system, and the one most commonly adopted, is to group the staff into small teams who have a responsibility for a particular part of a large site or, if the sites are smaller, all work in a geographical area. Usually the teams will be under the direction of skilled chargehands who will, hopefully, identify with the sites, regard them as 'their own' and get to know the users and the best way of achieving attractive results. The team will, of course, need to have the use of, or easy access to, a whole range of equipment and some of it may be relatively rarely used. As a result, modest, less efficient machines might be purchased to keep the capital costs down, e.g. by using a knapsack sprayer instead of a motorized one. The staff themselves will need to be more adaptable and highly trained and better able to organize their own work. However, for most, the variety of work, the achievement of a finished product and the contact with the people who use the site, provide a strong incentive for them to work consistently and to take pride in their work. This in turn reduces the need for close supervision so that the overall costs are unlikely to be significantly higher from the more efficient 'production-line' approach.

The size of the team is particularly important and generally needs to be kept as small as possible. The cynic might say that the more people in the team, the more people there are to talk to and therefore the output per person falls as the team size increases. This certainly appears to be the case where very small sites are concerned, and even on larger areas staff will tend to congregate and even get in each other's way if they are not very well organized. In practice a mobile team with a van and trailer, moving from site to site, should preferably consist of only two people. The travelling time is kept to a reasonable minimum and, if they are well matched, the pair should be able to cope with the majority of the tasks. However, if one goes sick or is absent, his partner may not be able to load and unload heavy equipment singlehanded and, for safety reasons, it is not desirable that one person works entirely on his own. To overcome this problem a three-person team is preferable; they can all sit in the front of a 'Transit'-type van and still function well when one person is absent (annual holidays alone can make this a reality for a quarter or more of the time).

In any maintenance organization these basic principles are likely to be adopted to suit the particular needs of the sites. Thus in a shire county with responsibility for rural schools, it is usual to have a small mobile team based at each secondary school. One person will probably spend most of his or her time on the large 'base' site with the other two travelling to and maintaining the satellite primary schools and other sites. The team will normally carry out all the operations on 'their' sites, with the exception of gang-mowing which will be done by a specialist tractor driver, sometimes mowing the large grass areas on the sites of two or more teams. In very rural areas, where the travelling distances are large, it may not be economic to drive the tractor from site to site and so the mobile team will carry their 'own' ride-on triple mower with them and mow the playing fields as well.

Supervision

One of the advantages of the team system is that, with good staff, it will virtually run itself and the foreman or supervisor really only has to concentrate on the teams who do not seem to be getting round their work on time. However, even some skilled gardeners and groundsmen often have difficulty in coping with the relative freedom of organizing their own work. Like many good weekend amateurs, they potter. In their enthusiasm to get the many things done, they flit from job to job, start many and finish few and at the worst, end up a nervous wreck. For those, and many others, an explicit programme of routine tasks can make all the difference so that they can work methodically through the day, dealing with the main priorities and coping with the rest as and when time allows. Often such programmes will come from a bonus incentive scheme, even printed by computer (see example, in appendix 5.I) but if this is not the case the simple expedient of writing down a list of jobs to be done at the start of each day, will keep the team working methodically. Even if the tasks seem insurmountable, the satisfaction of ticking off the jobs one by one can make it all seem, and actually be, possible.

The supervisor can prepare the job lists himself as a sort of daily instruction sheet, but many people will feel more committed to their own lists and it may be better for each chargehand to be encouraged to produce his own work programme. Even so the supervisor will need to vet them to ensure that the team are getting their priorities right and, of course, setting themselves reasonable work targets.

Bonus Incentive Schemes

Systems of work targeting, supervision and team working are all part of the process of motivating the staff, but one of the most commonly used motivators are bonus incentive schemes, particularly in the public sector of the landscape maintenance industry.

From the start of the industrial revolution, and probably well before that, employers have used bonus incentive schemes in some form or another as a means of encouraging their workforce to work harder and produce more. Probably the simplest form of all is a piecework payment where the worker is paid so much per 'piece' for each item of work produced. In a horticultural context a great deal of fruit-picking is usually paid for at so much per punnet or box. Many other forms of work are rewarded either wholly, or in part, on a piecework or commission basis, from factory workers at lathes, to insurance salesmen or icecream sellers.

All of these systems have several important things in common which can either be very useful to the employer, or sometimes, not entirely helpful. First of all, the incentive payments can act as a very powerful stimulus, particularly if they represent all, or a large part, of the workers' pay. This in turn means that the employer needs to have much less concern about supervising his workforce, making sure they start and finish on time and work at a reasonable pace through the day. He merely has to count the items produced and pay accordingly.

Checking the quality of the work can be rather more of a problem. Even workers paid by the hour will tend to skimp their job if the going gets tough. To do so is a human characteristic, in us all to a greater or lesser extent, no matter how conscientious we might be and particularly if we feel we have some sort of grudge against our employer (e.g. 'he doesn't pay me what I'm worth'). Piecework systems or incentives make the matter worse. The worker's livelihood depends on how many items he can get counted by the employer and that tends to become the overriding priority. The work is being done merely to produce money, not out of any sense of pride or personal fulfilment that would make the quality of output important. The employer therefore has to set very clear standards for what he wants and adopt effective measures to ensure that the quality is achieved. Unfortunately, this checking can frequently be the cause of conflict between the workers and manager.

An even greater source of conflict is the rate for the job. If the rate is too generous, the company makes a loss. If it is too low, the workers feel exploited and may well refuse the work, either by mass strike or simply by resigning. Fixing the rate for the job, therefore, often involves a good deal of 'horse-trading' between the two parties. It was possibly the need to try to resolve these conflicts that prompted the use of work study in payment systems.

Work Study

People working in local government could well be excused for thinking that work study and incentive schemes are much the same thing and certainly the two terms are popularly used synonymously. Work study is, however, the systematic study of work and operations and, although the results can be used for rate fixing in bonus incentive schemes, it does, in fact, have many more applications as a management tool. For simplicity its use in landscape management can be divided into two basic parts:

Method study
Time studies.

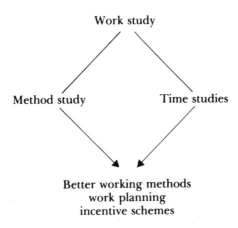

Work study
Method study   Time studies
Better working methods
work planning
incentive schemes

Method study analyses the individual operations that go into producing a particular finished piece of work and hopefully identifies any wasted or unnecessary operations, and any impediments in the process. It then arrives at a blueprint for the most efficient method of work. This form of study is particularly useful for repetitive industrial processes, combining, for instance, with ergonomics to ensure that work stations, tools and materials are easily and comfortably to hand. It has also been used in the design of horticultural packhouses and nurseries so that the movement of produce and packaging are kept to a minimum. It is valuable in a whole range of grounds maintenance tasks, for instance, in deciding on the relative merits of different types of machinery or for organizing itineraries and work programmes.

Time study is the more specific exercise of finding out how long a job takes and it is this information that is particularly valuable in planning both day-to-day work and the longer-term setting of manning levels, budget or tender prices. However, job times, if they are to be of any value, should be based on the most efficient working method and therefore some element of method study must always be a precursor to any time studies.

Standard Times

All of us are different in many ways and not the least in our pace of work. Also, our individual working rate will vary according to the time of day, from day to day, and even according to our moods, state of health or general inclination.

To overcome these problems and arrive at a standard time that can be applied to a number of different people, the work study practitioners have arrived at a concept of 'rating' by which they measure the motivation and effort an individual puts into an operation. Such ideas are often difficult for the layman to appreciate, but they have proved workable in practice and they depend at their core on the definition of standard working which in British Standard 3138:1969 is defined as:

> The rate of output which qualified workers will naturally achieve without over exertion, as an average, over the working day or shift, provided they adhere to the specified method and provided they are motivated to apply themselves to their work.

Several things are inferred in this definition.

1. It is not the rate of the fastest worker; just the rate of the average.
2. It is the rate of the average *qualified* worker in that particular workforce, i.e. one who is accepted as skilled

and competent in the particular job, presumably by his colleagues as well as his employer. This means that a standard time cannot necessarily be transferred from one workforce to another. If Scottish green keepers are especially skilled in comparison with their southern counterparts, their standard time for mowing a green will be so much the lesser. In practice, however, these differences are likely to be very small with much greater variation due to type of machinery, type of grass, or even the weather.

3. It is the rate of working that can be sustained throughout the *whole* of the working day and not just for a brief spell while the foreman is watching.

The skill of assessing working effort, or rating, takes a good deal of careful training but even the layman can distinguish between obviously fast and slow rates and score them, say on a scale of 1–10. What the trained and experienced work study officer can do is make much finer judgements down to a few percentage points on a 1–100 scale.

Standard working under the British Standards definition is set at 100 and as a guide this is equivalent to walking at 4 mph – a fairly brisk pace but one which a fit and experienced walker can keep up for a working day with adequate rest stops. Walking at only 3 mph is rather more leisurely and on the same scale represents a rating of 0.75.

Using this system of rating the basic time for, say, mowing a $1000m^2$ of lawn, can be established by timing the job on a number of different occasions and multiplying it by the observed rating as shown below:

Observed time	Rating		Basic time
40 minutes	110/100	=	44 minutes
50 minutes	90/100	=	45 minutes
60 minutes	80/100	=	48 minutes

These basic times can then be averaged and obviously the greater the number of separate studies the more reliable will be the time.

Finally, a rest and contingency allowance must be added to this basic time so that it is a genuine time that can be sustained throughout the working day. The rest allowance depends on the nature of the work and is usually left very much to the judgement of the work study officer. Common amounts are 5 per cent for a relatively light job, say up to 15 per cent for heavy manual work like digging. Contingencies also vary but the allowance will usually be based on what interruptions to the work are observed during the studies. If, for instance, a hedge-trimming machine has to be continually unblocked or resharpened that would be included in the contingency time for the job. Thus, adding the contingency and rest allowances to the basic time gives the standard time for the job (see Figure 5.1).

One further item that needs to be accounted for is the initial getting out of the equipment, preparing it for work (checking oil, adjusting, filling with fuel, etc.) and storing it away again at the end of the job. The time for this is likely to be the same whatever the size of the job and so it is best kept as a separate item as shown in the example in Figure 5.1 (Preparation and Disposal). However, although this procedure is more likely to be mathematically correct, it is an extra complication and a more simple arrangement is to add a fixed percentage to the standard time to allow for the preparation and storing away of the equipment. For example, for the mowing shown in Figure 5.1, it might be reasonable to assume that the work will normally be done in half-day blocks and so for every four hours of work the preparation time will represent $\frac{12 \text{ minutes}}{480 \text{ minutes}} = 2.5$ per cent. Thus the standard time would be increased by 2.5 per cent.

Making a Standard Time

If standard times are to be used as a basis for a bonus incentive system, as distinct from more approximate work planning, it is essential that they are as accurate as possible and, just as importantly, are regarded as credible by the staff who are going to work to them. The following procedures are therefore recommended.

1. *Specify the task*. This is an essential prerequisite and the definition should clearly state the expected end result

Operation	*Grass cutting cricket squares and tennis courts*				

Equipment   34″ Atco Cylinder Mower
Width of cut   34″
Reel:
   No. of Cutters   6
   Cuts per yard   81
   Adj. to height of cut $\frac{1}{2}″ - \frac{7}{8}″$
Overall width   41″

Ancillary equipment   Petrol, Oil, Oil Can, Grease Gun, Grass Box, Sheeting and Hand Tools.

Method   Check area and remove any surface obstructions. Cut grass ensuring minimum overlap, spread cuttings in grass box, check and adjust cutting height and/or blade, refuel as required. Empty full grass box to sheeting at work place and dispose of cuttings in sheeting on completion of operations.

Additional for tennis courts. Place aside and replace nets to facilitate grass cutting.

Preparation   As per Grass Cutting (Boxed) Amenity Lawns Code No. 126.

Disposal   As per Grass Cutting (Boxed) Amenity Lawns Code No. 126.

	B.M.'S	C.A.%	R.A.%	S.M.V.	PER	Code
Operation	2.05	15	15	2.71	100 sq.*	110
Preparation	5.66	5	15	6.82		
Disposal	3.82	5	15	4.61		
				11.43	Occ.	126
Additional Value	1.50	15	18	2.10	Court.	

Figure 5.1 *Sample job specification and standard minute value*

(e.g. lawn neatly mown in straight alternate lines), the equipment to be used and some indication of method of working (see Figure 5.1).

2. *Inform the staff and involve the 'workers' representative.* No time studies should be carried out until the staff have been told about the nature and purpose of the exercise. Staff cooperation is essential for reliable results and in many cases there may need to be a formal agreement between the management and the workforce, or the

union, before the studies can begin. The individuals who are studied should have the exercise explained to them and, if possible, given some indication of the results of their particular study.

The involvement of a workers' representative (appointed by the staff) can be of great value in gaining the confidence of the workforce and can be a source of detailed information about the various practical problems of the task. Ideally the workers' representative should be able to carry out his own independent studies of the task, under the guidance of an experienced work study officer, and given some appropriate training and practice (typically 3–4 days).

3.   *Make some preliminary method studies.* These are important to ensure that the workforce are using appropriate working methods and that the end-result matches the task specification. These early studies should best be applied to several different people and if this reveals that the methods of working vary, it may be necessary to redefine the task.

4.   *Carry out the time-studies.* At least ten separate studies should be undertaken of each task and they should be spread as widely as possible to include different staff, times of year, soil and weather conditions. If the results are all within a reasonable spread of the mean, say ± 10 per cent, they can all be used within the standard time. They may, however, show a much wider spread and a decision will then have to be made about the extent to which tasks carried out under different conditions can be grouped together. Grass mowing, for instance, is usually more difficult in the lush growing season of late spring, but much easier in late summer. Separate standard times could be set for mowing thick damp or thin dry grass, but the definition between the two could be very difficult. Therefore, for sake of simplicity, it is usual to try to establish average times on the understanding that they will represent the total workload throughout a season; underestimating it at difficult times but with compensating overestimates for the easier parts of the year.

Such averaging is, however, less acceptable where factors such as soil, level of use or frequency of interruptions are constantly greater or lesser on a given site. For instance, digging on a heavy clay soil will vary in its difficulty according to the time of year (mostly from just possible to not at all), but will nearly always be significantly harder than on a light sandy soil. Averaging these two extremes is unlikely to be satisfactory and may only produce a time which is unrealistic for both. Cultivating less extreme soil types could be reasonably averaged and, indeed, may be the only practical alternative to establishing rather complicated separate specifications for each soil type.

Transplanting of Standard Times and Using Estimates

Many local authorities in the United Kingdom have established their own lists of standard times (see Chapter 2 for examples), and properly used, they can be of great use to their managers. However, accurate times are nearly always specific to the circumstances of that particular employer and workforce and can therefore only be used elsewhere, with accuracy, if the circumstances are similar and if a full and detailed specification for the task is available.

Various national lists of job times have been drawn up, the earliest being prepared by LAMSAC (Local Authorities Management Services and Computer Committee). A more recent compilation has been made by the Groundwork Trust (Making the Most of Greenspace. Vol. II, Output Guides for Landscape Management). Both these lists give good indications of job times and as such they are a very valuable guide for estimating annual maintenance costs or manning levels, for example. However, these lists and the tasks specifications in them are not sufficiently detailed to use as the basis of a bonus incentive scheme and would need to be used with some caution as a base for pricing contract tenders. Any employer who wishes to use work study-based standard times in these ways, therefore has to make arrangements to have the firm's employees properly studied and timed.

Task	Time (hours)	April to June Frequency	Total time	July to September Frequency	Total time
Mowing large lawns	8	10	80	8	64
Mowing small lawns	12	15	180	12	144
Mowing banks	4	4	16	3	12
Mowing bulb areas	10	—	—	1	10
Edge clipping	4	6	24	6	24
Herbaceous border hoe and tidy	3	6	18	4	12
Clip internal hedges	25	1	25	1	25
Contingency	4 (per week)		52		52
Total			395		343
Average per week			30.4		26.4

Figure 5.2   *Approximate calculation of workload*

The costs of this can be considerable, depending on the range of work undertaken and the variations in conditions. Thus, to some extent, the need for study work will be greater for a large workforce, but not on a *pro rata* basis with even a small workforce needing a good deal of study to establish a basic list of standard times. The costs can be reduced by only concentrating on the more regular and frequent operations but it is still likely that the study work would involve 2–3 man-years of work study officer time to prepare a reliable list of times for most aspects of grounds maintenance work. Thereafter, any list needs regular review and updating, but the initial 'capital' cost is likely to be considerable for a small workforce in terms of cost per employee. This factor alone, therefore, makes work study-based bonus incentive schemes unsuitable for small grounds maintenance organizations where a more approximate productivity agreement would be more sensible. This type of agreement might be suitable for the staff of a large ornamental garden where the workloads could be calculated using some loosely estimated times for the main tasks as shown in Figure 5.2.

The individual times can be estimated from previous time-sheet records, or even by negotiation with the employer and staff, but, provided the times are reasonably estimated, the total figure will give some basis for negotiating a productivity agreement. For example, a 10 per cent reduction in staffing, through not filling a vacancy, could be rewarded with an appropriate bonus to the remaining staff if they maintained the previous standards with reduced working hours.

These simple types of scheme can be suitable for a small workforce but they are very unlikely to achieve the much greater savings and increases in productivity that are likely to flow from a properly researched work study-based scheme.

Incentive and Productivity Schemes

Two main types of incentive schemes have been adopted by local authorities for grounds maintenance, described under the generic titles of PBR (Payment by Results) and Measured Day Work.

In PBR schemes the work carried out by each individual or small group of staff is measured at the end of each week, in terms of standard minutes or hours, and this is divided by the attendance hours to give a measure of performance e.g.

$$\frac{\text{work completed (standard hours)} \times 100}{\text{Attendance hours}}$$
$$= \text{performance.}$$

Bonus is then paid according to the performance achieved, usually on the basis that a standard performance of 100 attracts a bonus of one-third of normal earnings and no bonus at all is earned at 75 performance. Intermediate bonus earnings are assessed according to the straight-line relationship in Figure 5.3. In some schemes a geared system of bonus calculation may be used as shown by the dotted line in Figure 5.3. This is usually adopted to provide some incentive at the lower levels of performance with a corresponding tail-off at the upper reaches. A cut-off point is usually built in (at 125 performance or two-thirds bonus) to protect the general health and safety of the employees.

'Measured day work' schemes are based on the same perfor-

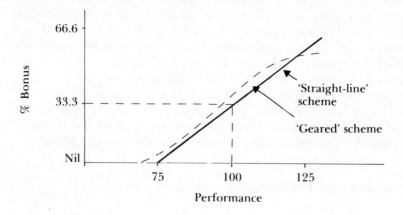

Figure 5.3   *Bonus and performance*

mance earning ratios shown in Figure 5.3 but the average rate
of working is first agreed between the manager and employees
and then each employee, or group, are required to complete
prearranged work programmes based on the agreed performance rate. The work programmes are designed to fill the
working hours and, provided they regularly complete those
programmes, are paid a regular fixed rate of bonus.

The PBR scheme provides the most positive incentives to the
employee but at the same time gives strong incentives to rush or
skimp the work and can cause arguments within the workforce
over the allocation of 'easy' and 'difficult' tasks (Skilled tasks,
e.g. pruning, are often more difficult for achieving high bonus
rates.) In addition, the employer has relatively little control over
the volume of work that is done and can be under pressure to
increase the frequencies of operations in order to maintain
bonus earnings. Such problems can be overcome by gradual
adjustment of the workloads/manning levels but a more important problem can stem from the volume of detailed recording
that is needed to measure each man's weekly output.

In measured day work schemes the incentive to the individual
is much less and it falls much more to the supervision to ensure
that the work rate is maintained. However, the employer has

greater control over the volume of work that is completed, incentives to skimp are lessened and the recording and paper-work can be reduced.

The choice between one type of scheme or another is very much a matter for the employer and workforce to agree. It is also possible to have schemes that combine elements of the two main types but, in general, the PBR scheme is most useful for situations where there is a high volume of a few relatively unskilled tasks, e.g. verge mowing and edging. Conversely, the measured day work scheme tends to have advantage where there is the need for a larger number of different tasks of varying skills, e.g. sports field maintenance or ornamental gardens.

Tender-led and Total Target Incentive Schemes

In PBR schemes the incentives are concentrated on the completion of individual tasks. The tendency is less marked with measured day work schemes where the emphasis is more towards completing a series of operations that will achieve an overall finish or standard of maintenance. This fact can therefore be recognized by setting a total target of work hours (a budget time) for the upkeep of each site in each four-week period of the year and including allowances in the budget time to take account of wet and other lost time and the travelling to and from the site. Any extra work, over and above the routine maintenance, is ordered by the employer as it becomes necessary so that the performance calculation (the basis for bonus payments) is:

$$\text{Performance} = \frac{\text{Budget hours} + \text{hours for completed works orders}}{\text{attendance hours}}$$

This calculation is based on the assumption that the site or sites have been maintained to the specified standard and that any deficiencies in that respect are put right without any extra allowances.

This system has a number of advantages:

1. Staff are encouraged to use their skill and judgement in

      deciding what work is necessary to achieve the standard (as in a performance specification under a contract).

2.   Administration is relatively simple and supervision can concentrate on the task of ensuring that the specified standards are achieved.
3.   Staff are encouraged to make the best use of wet weather and to minimize lost time and unproductive travelling.

One further advantage is that the total costs to the employer are relatively fixed and directly linked to the achievement of the particular standard of maintenance. This in turn means that the system is well suited to contract systems where the payments to the contractor, and in turn the staff, depends on satisfying the contract specification. In these circumstances, the budget hours can be based, to a greater or lesser extent, on the tender price on which a contract is based (tender-led). In the first instance, the budget hours should be based on work study or other standard times but then modified as necessary in order to achieve a competitive price. The variations from the standard times need to be done with great care and judgement and, as much as possible, with the agreement of the workforce. For instance, consistently low pricing of the tenders may well win the jobs but at the cost of reduced earnings for the staff. However, the use of tender-led incentives does help to ensure that any bonus payments do reflect the income received from the client.

Sickness, Unmeasured Work, etc.

Under any form of bonus incentive scheme there has to be arrangement for wet and other times when work is not possible and for time lost through sickness, industrial injuries or other reasons. All the factors can be negotiated separately for each employer but there are certain conventions that have generally been adopted in local authorities. The majority of these are included in the Code of Guiding Principles and Practice for Work Study Based Incentive Schemes for Local Authority Services (Manual Workers).

    In general the main arrangements are as follows:

1. Wet and lost time are only paid at the base rate or the average bonus rate for team or employee at the time (limits on total wet and lost time may be set under Total Target or Tender led schemes).
2. Time spent on unmeasured work is only paid at the base rate or at the average bonus rate if it would be unpractical to fix standard times.
3. Time spent on training and approved union activities is paid at average bonus rate.
4. No bonus is paid for sick-time but it is payable on sick-time resulting from an injury at work.

An example of an agreement on these matters is shown in Appendix 5.II.

FORECAST OF PLANNED MAINTENANCE FOR HERNE CEPS

SITE No. 06-285-2-0

CODE	SCHEDULE OF OPERATIONS	TOTAL QUANTITY	HOURS PER WEEK – BY WEEK NUMBER											
			1	2	3	4	5	6	7	8	9	10	11	12
378	MOW AREA (20" ANTELOPE)	1858		1.73		1.73	1.73	1.73	1.73	1.73	1.73	1.73	1.73	1.73
380														
381														
391	MOW ROUND OBSTRUCTION/TREE	40		0.15		0.15	0.15	0.15	0.15	0.15	0.15	0.15	0.15	0.15
393														
394														
419	ROTARY MOW AREA	6		0.17				0.17				0.17		
420														
421														
463	FLYMO BANKS	347		0.87		0.87		0.87		0.87		0.87		
506	CLIP BORDER EDGES	59	0.36			0.36			0.36			0.36		
618	MOW C/P CRICKET STRIP (20" BXD)	1				0.34	0.34	0.34	0.34	0.34	0.34	0.34	0.34	0.34
619														
1127	SET OUT ROUNDERS	5												
1128	RE-MARK ROUNDERS	5		2.83										
1129	SET OUT ROUNDERS	5												
1130	RE-MARK ROUNDERS	5			0.58	0.58	0.58	0.58	0.58	0.58	0.58	0.58	0.58	0.58
1185	REMOVE 5-A-SIDE POSTS	2	1.00											
1200	RE-MARK 5-A-SIDE	2	0.47	0.47	0.47	0.47	0.47	0.47	0.47	0.47	0.47	0.47	0.47	0.47
1275	SET OUT 75M 8-LANE TRACK	1						1.95*						
1276	RE-MARK 75M 8-LANE TRACK	1							0.38*	0.38*	0.38*	0.38*	0.38*	0.38*
1650	MARK DAY WICKETS	1				0.56	0.56	0.56	0.56	0.56	0.56	0.56	0.56	0.56
1851	TAKEN DOWN FOOTBALL POSTS	2		2.00										
2050	SPRAY FENCE LINES	672	1.24											
2051	SPRAY TREE BASES	38	0.13											
2052	SPRAY BUILDING LINES	315	0.46											
2058	CHECK TREE STAKES & TIES	29	0.48											
2061	SPRAY ROSES	34				0.25				0.25				
2087	SURROUNDS – INSP/SPOT WEED/TIDY	1					0.39				0.39			
2663	HEDGE <1.7M TOP & 2 SIDES (ARROW)	27										0.57	0.38	
	TOTAL PRODUCTIVE HOURS		4.14	8.22	1.05	5.32	4.23	6.83	4.58	5.34	4.61	6.19	4.59	4.22
	CARRIED/BROUGHT FORWARD													
	DEFERRED/CANCELLED WORK													
	SITE VARIANCE TOTAL													

Appendix 5.I *Sample of a computer-printed work schedule*

118

Appendix 5.II*
Bonus Scheme Agreement: Part I

INTRODUCTION

THIS WORK SPECIFICATION applies to operations carried out by the direct labour force under the direction of the County Estates Officer & Valuer.

The Department accepts the provisions of the Code of Guiding Principles for Work Study in Local Authorities' Services issued by the National Joint Council for Local Authorities' Services (Manual Workers) dated 16th December, 1965, and, in addition to the general conditions agreed in this Part of the Work Specification, will be guided by the Code in any other matters of policy or interpretation arising from the operation of the schemes.

The specification is in two parts.
Part I
General conditions applying to all schemes.
Part II
Particular conditions applying to the scheme.

PART I

1.   BONUS
1.1.   The scheme, based on Work Study, is designed so that the average man experienced in the work will have the opportunity to earn, in addition to his basic rate of pay, a bonus at standard performance equivalent to one third of his basic rate of pay. The basic rate of pay is the national, provincial or local agreed rate for the job, including any plus rate for skill or responsibility and, where appropriate, service supplement.
1.2.   It is recognised that the scheme will embody this principle in the manner best suited to the types of work performed by the specified classes of employees and to ensure this specific provision may be made in Part Two of this specification relating to:-

*Based on a document originally prepared by Kent County Council the assessment of performance by individuals or by groups;

the period over which targets are to be set and performance is to be assessed (e.g. by measured day work or other task-based scheme);

the starting level for payment of bonus;

devices to stabilise payment of bonus.

2.   HOW THE SCHEME WORKS

The substance of the provisions which follow in paragraphs 2.1.–3.4. will be preserved throughout all schemes. If because of the nature of the scheme it would be desirable to modify the way in which they should be administered this will be specified in part II.

2.1.   Each employee or team will complete a record showing how his or their time has been spent on working and waiting. The records when signed by the supervisor are used to calculate bonus.

2.2.   Bonus may be earned on all work for which standard times or temporary targets have been compiled i.e. on measured work. Such time includes allowances for rest and personal needs, minor interruptions and delays and may include, where applicable, travel times and site allowances.

2.4.   Time spent in travelling to work for the commencement of the day and from the work site at the end of the day is not included.

2.5.   Bonus is calculated by adding the standard times earned over the week or lesser periods of working and relating them to the time taken to do the work in accordance with the scheme described in Part 2.

2.6.   Bonus is calculated daily, or for other agreed period, and paid weekly, normally one week in arrear.

2.7.   In order to safeguard health and quality of work and to avoid the abuse of machinery and equipment the maximum bonus rate will be that quoted in Part 2.

3.   TIME NOT ON BONUS

3.1.   It may not be possible to work on bonus all the time.

3.2.   Unmeasured Work

It is implicit in a bonus scheme based on work study, that unmeasured work should be kept to a minimum. Bonus is not paid for this, subject to the following:-

3.2.1. Where an employee, normally engaged on measured work, is required to carry out productive work of an unusual nature which is necessarily left unmeasured his earnings shall not be adversely affected, provided a satisfactory standard of output is achieved. In such cases average bonus, as defined in paragraph 3.2.3 below will be paid for all hours so spent.

3.2.2. During the first three months of the scheme average bonus payments for unmeasured work shall not exceed $16\frac{2}{3}$ per cent. of the basic wage, but thereafter this limit will not apply.

3.2.3. After a trial period of three months bonus will be paid for unmeasured work in excess of six hours in any one week at the rate of the average bonus per attendance hour earned during the two weeks preceding the week in which the unmeasured work occurred.

3.3. Lost Time

This occurs when a man or team is prevented from working for period of ten minutes or more. Periods of time under this heading will be paid for at the basic rate.

4. ARBITRATION

Difficulties arising from the introduction or operation of work study or incentive schemes which cannot be settled locally may, at the request of either side, be referred for conciliation.

5. QUALITY OF WORK

Bonus is not paid for sub-standard work or unsafe methods of working.

Checks will continue to be made to ensure that quality and safety standards are being maintained.

6. GENERAL CONDITIONS

Investigations may be made into methods, degree of specialisation, materials, equipment and working conditions with the object of introducing improvements. Targets may be altered, at the request of either side, when there is:-

a change in method, degree of specialisation, materials, equipment or working condition;

an error or miscalculation.

Any proposed change will be explained to all concerned through the established procedure.

7.   CONDITIONS OF SERVICE

Except as set out in this specification, the conditions of service of employees within its scope shall continue to be those applying at the date of this specification.

8.   DURATION OF SCHEMES

The period of notice required to be given by either the Department or the Employee's Side of intention to terminate the specified schemes by negotiation shall be three months.

Bonus Scheme Agreement: Part II

CONTENTS

APPENDICES

II.   Summary of Standard Minute Values and Allowances

III.   Examples of Team Work Programme

IV.   Vehicle Inspection Report.

1.   *Introduction*
1.1.   This Part II Work specification describes the work, particular conditions and method of bonus payment to be applied to the operation of the work study based incentive scheme for grounds staff employed for the maintenance of the grounds of the County Council properties.

1.2.   This specification should be read in conjunction with the Part I specification agreed between the County Council and the Unions in June 1969, and subsequently accepted by the grounds staff of the seven separate maintenance groups.

1.3.   In the same way, this Part II specification will be submitted for acceptance to the grounds staff of each group so that the application and control of the scheme may be carried out on a group basis.

1.4.   The scheme will operate for a trial period of a full maintenance year (12 months) for each group, after which time it will be subject to review and agreement between the County Council and the men concerned.

1.5.   Any queries by the men which arise from the scheme may be raised with management by grounds staff or by the Trade Union representatives.

1.6.   It is the County Council's intention to negotiate with the Unions on any problem arising from the implementation of the scheme which cannot be settled at local level.

1.7.   The scheme will come into operation in Division as from

2.   *The Bonus Incentive Scheme*
2.1.   The scheme is designed so that each workman will receive a fixed weekly bonus relative to attendance hours in return for completing a planned programme of work at the accepted quality standard and with due

regard to safe working methods. Bonus will be paid to Union Stewards while conducting approved duties.

2.2. For the purpose of this scheme the annual work programme has been divided into 13 four-weekly periods from April to the following March. In this document the term "Summer months" relates to the first 8 periods running approximately from April to October inclusive.

2.3. The intention is that the bonus for the summer months will ultimately be $33\frac{1}{3}\%$ of basic weekly wage, including service supplement and chargehand's allowance, where applicable; and that the work programme will be set on 100 B.S.I. performance over a 40 hour week.

During the winter months, when the routine maintenance work is necessarily much reduced, the bonus will ultimately be 20% of basic wage, plus appropriate allowances, and the work programme will be set on a maximum of 90 B.S.I. performance for a 40 hour week.

2.4. Where considerations of group overmanning preclude the introduction of the scheme at 100 B.S.I. performance level it is agreed that, where appropriate, the scheme will be implemented at 90 B.S.I. performance level for the summer months and at 85 B.S.I. performance level for the winter months. In these circumstances the fixed bonus levels would be reduced to 20% and 15% respectively.

2.5. Arising from changes of method and equipment, the work will be studied to determine the effect on standard minute values and the work programme. Where necessary, revised work programmes will be issued subject to negotiations with the Unions.

2.6. The manpower, disposition and work programme of each group will normally be reviewed on an annual basis. Improvements in productivity and changes in manning levels will be negotiated and agreed changes will be incorporated in the scheme to take effect from the ensuing maintenance year e.g. the following April.

2.7. The work values included in this specification have been set on equipment and methods of work currently in use (Set out as Appendix I). The range of work operations are set out in the "Code of Practice for Maintenance of Grounds" which has been issued to all chargehands and has been used in conjunction with the site plan, quantified information on site layout and facilities, method specifications and work values to produce work schedules for each maintained site.

2.8.   From the site schedules and with the addition of team travelling allowances and other appropriate allowances (See Appendix II), work programmes have been devised for each team or groundsman in respect of the routine grounds maintenance work (See examples as Appendix III).

2.9.   Since it is not possible to programme 40 hours of routine maintenance work per man for every week of the year, an amount of time called "balancing time" will be shown in the work programmes of all teams.

2.10.   This balancing time will tend to vary from week to week and also, to a lesser extent, between team and team. In this connection, as a fixed bonus will be paid relative to the attendance hours of each man, the incidence of unabsorbed balancing time within each team will be available to supervisors for the allocation of other tasks not included in the routine maintenance programme.

2.11.   Among other tasks are the following:-
Additional grounds maintenance work requested by a school;
planting schemes and minor construction works;
the upkeep of certain pavilions;
the upkeep of grounds staff depots;
snow clearing and leaf sweeping;
rubbish clearance on newly acquired sites;
emergency work on sites arising from inclement weather.

2.12.   Minor items of work requested by school Head Teachers may be carried out at the discretion of the chargehand provided it can be accommodated within the unabsorbed balancing time and that the Foreman is informed as soon as possible after the event. Other work not shown on the work programme may only be undertaken on the instructions of the Foreman or Superintendent.

2.13. Overtime working may be necessary at certain times of the year. In principle, it will only be required for the purpose of carrying out essential work that cannot be accommodated within the unabsorbed balancing time or by a re-arrangement of the weekly work programme.

2.14. In the event at any time of the agreed level of performance and or quality not being achieved, the County Council may, after examination of the circumstances and consultation with the Union Steward withhold bonus payments.

2.15. Bonus will be calculated weekly and paid in arrears, together with allowances in accordance with current practice.

3. *Organisation of Grounds Staff*

3.1. In continuance of current policy, most members of the grounds staff will be allocated to teams under the control of a chargehand. Others e.g. tractor and lorry drivers and detached groundsmen, will normally work as individuals under the control of a foreman.

3.2. Changes in allocation may be made from time to time to accommodate, for example, long term sickness or annual leave, or for the performance of special work requiring a larger team or any other change within contract of service.

4. *Work Records*

4.1. Chargehands, detached groundsmen, tractor and lorry drivers, will be issued with work programmes. They will be required to record the details of non-completed tasks and/or additional work not shown on the programme. The required signature on each daily work programme will signify that the specified work has been completed to the accepted standard of quality.

4.2. Drivers will be required to complete vehicle inspection reports and, where appropriate, drivers record sheets. (See Appendix V).

5. *Holidays*

5.1. Leave arrangements will be the subject of separate negotiation.

6. *Sickness*
6.1. Bonus will not be paid for sick leave.

7. *Trainees*
7.1. Trainee groundsmen will be employed as at present on a variety of tasks and may be moved from team to team to gain a wide work experience. The presence of a trainee will help to compensate for sickness or leave in a team but in the case of fully manned teams the presence of a trainee would not result in any reduction of bonus payment to the team.
7.2. Bonus payments to trainees will be based on basic wages as follows:

> 1st year   No bonus payment
> 2nd year $\frac{1}{2}$ bonus
> 3rd year full bonus

Bonus will be paid for attendance hours, including those spent on day release and other training sessions.

The level of Bonus Payments will be the subject of further review in consultation with the Trade Unions.

8. *Supernumeraries*
8.1. Supernumerary grounds staff will not be included in the bonus incentive scheme and wherever possible will be employed on simple grounds maintenance tasks, additional to the team work programme. The establishment of supernumeraries is ten (10).
8.2. The attachment of a supernumerary to a team will not, of itself, affect the team's bonus payments and, as at present, would only be arranged with the agreement of the team concerned.

9. *Examples of Bonus Calculations - Excluded*

10. *Conclusion*
10.1. Nothing in the foregoing agreement shall preclude the right of management to negotiate for changes in the operation of schemes should equipment, conditions or other circumstances alter at any time.

10.2.   Non legally binding clause
Both parties accept that this agreement is binding in honour between them but both expressly agree that it is not intended to constitute a legally enforceable agreement. It is further agreed that the parties to the agreement will use their best endeavours to ensure that the spirit and intention of the agreement is honoured at all times.

Agreed on behalf of the County Council

Date ....

Agreed on behalf of the Unions.

Date ....

Chapter 6

STAFF WELFARE AND SAFETY

Safety saves lives, injury and lost production. A generous welfare package generates high morale and high productivity. To offer both is seen by some employers as an unnecessary expense and reduced to the minimum possible. However a careful look at certain major High Street retailers will show that time, effort and money spent on staff care is not wasted.

The Health and Safety at Work (etc.) Act 1974 is the single most significant piece of recent legislation in the field of safety placing a broad general duty of care upon employers, employees, manufacturers of industrial products, the self-employed and the occupiers of buildings where people work.

- It is the duty of employers to ensure as far as is reasonably practicable the safety of their employees at work, for example, by maintaining safe plant, safe systems of work and safe premises;
- on employees to take reasonable care of the health and safety of themselves while at work;
- on the self-employed persons, to carry on their business in such a way as to ensure, so far as reasonably practicable, that they do not put at risk their own health and safety; and
- on employers, self-employed and employees not to put at risk the health and safety of third parties.

Under the Act anyone who intentionally or recklessly interferes with or misuses anything provided under a safety require-

129

ment of law in the interests of health, safety or welfare, is liable to prosecution.

The enforcement of the Act is the responsibility of the Health and Safety Executive and local authorities. However, powers are not limited to prosecution with improvement and prohibition notices being part of an Inspector's powers. The HSE is available for advice and guidance in all aspects of safety in the work place and the application of the relevant sections of the HSAW Act.

To ensure that safety is taken seriously at all levels in the organization, a clearly defined policy is required. This should be in the form of a general statement of intent outlining the overall philosophy to the management of health and safety; coupled with a clear definition of who is responsible for what within the organization. How the policy is to be monitored, the operation of any safety representative and committees and how individual job descriptions should include health and safety responsibilities should be identified. These two represent static elements of the policy, the dynamic element is the actual implementation via safety training, accident reporting and investigation, safe systems of work, fire safety, protective equipment and clothing, welfare considerations, etc. This section requires clear descriptions of procedures which can easily be understood by all levels of staff and which avoid petty bureaucracy. All matters of safety policy or procedure should be seen to be issued, and backed, at the highest managerial level and quickly brought to the attention of all employees. The commitment to safety among a workforce, unless in a particularly hazardous environment, is not usually high and the design of posters, textbooks and training sessions needs to be the best possible standard if the desired result is to be achieved.

In spite of all the efforts put in to drawing up a policy and disseminating information, accidents do happen at work. The collection of accident data serves to monitor the overall success of a health and safety policy. The type of accident, why and how it happened, together with the length of any absence from work, as a result need to be recorded. Accident books for recording each occurrence, however small, should be readily available. Analysis of the data can reveal trends and enable preventative measures, e.g. specific training or changes in work practices, to be developed. The cost of accidents to the organization should also be worked out, together with the cost of preventative measures to enable a manager to plan any improvements to the safety levels in his group. The allocation of a cash value to accidents rather than a blank statement of frequency of occurrence is likely significantly to assist in the aim of accident reduction.

Reliance solely on the financial penalties incurred due to accidents is not sufficient. Where possible accidents should be designed out of work systems. This requires careful analysis of work procedures to ensure that premises, plant, processes and materials used are safe and that protective clothing, etc., is adequate. Accidents happen to people – the human aspects of the organization – and they should be trained and motivated to avoid risk. The machinery, plant and equipment should be of sound design and correctly maintained. Materials should be the best possible and safe during the operation of the job and as finished products. In addition, the working environment should be the most congenial possible. All these linked together can help to limit accidents.

A happy, well-motivated workforce is likely to be more vigilant towards safety and more productive. An important element of the measures needed to bring about this state of affairs is the provision of good welfare facilities. This usually takes the form of a 'depot'. This can vary from a large unit housing the local/central manager, administrative staff, main stores, etc. and functioning as the central control point down to a domestic garage-sized unit occupied by a single person. Whatever the size the depot should provide suitable washing and toilet facilities, i.e. a WC and piped hot and cold running water together with a washbasin, soap and clean towels. These facilities will need to cater for a number of people employed and take into account the mix of sexes in the workforce. In larger depots a messroom should be available to provide a separate area for taking meals and rest periods. Space may not permit this level of provision in small units, however staff should have access to an area divided off in some way from machinery, tools, etc. in which to eat. Where staff are mobile covering a number of small geographically discrete sites the vehicle used becomes the 'depot' and should have adequate space in which to rest, eat or take shelter from the elements. The number, type and size of depots required is an important consideration for any organization. The cost of providing a new, purpose-built main depot of 265 square metres of garage space together with 95 square metres of office, storage and messroom facilities may cost about £100,000, while a single unit providing 21 square metres of garage with a small messroom and toilet of 10 square metres can cost £20,000. The rental cost for similar-sized buildings will vary according to location but for the larger depot may be £10,500 per annum and £1,200 for the smaller.

Once acquired, depots need to be maintained, equipped with furniture, telephones, etc., regularly inspected to ensure they are safe places in which to work, inspected by the local fire authority, etc. The cost of depots is therefore a major overhead and can be equivalent to between £700 and £900 per man per year. Monetary savings can easily be identified and made by reducing the level and quality of depot provision whereas the lost production due to lack of staff morale cannot. The balance between under- and over-provision is not easy to achieve but it is essential to the smooth running of the system.

The depot provides the daily base but staff require personal protection while undertaking their day-to-day duties, in particular, those which are potentially hazardous, such as the use of pesticides and chain saws. Basic protective clothing such as steel toecapped boots or shoes (BS 1870: 1976–81), wellingtons, overalls and perhaps an anorak/donkey jacket may be provided. Such a set would cost in the region of £45 and require replacement every 2–3 years. The application of pesticides and the safety provisions to apply are now covered by the Food and Environment Protection Act 1985, Pesticides Regulations 1986 and the Code of Practice for the Use of Approved Pesticides in Amenity Area 1988 which comprehensively regulate the use of pesticides and give detailed guidelines on storage in depots and protective clothing required as well as staff training. In brief, the minimum protective clothing operators require when handling concentrate is a face shield, overall and protective gloves.

The clothing must always fit, be appropriate to the job and where necessary meet the requirements of the Poisonous Substances in Agriculture Regulations 1984. (The use of chemicals is also governed by the Deposit of Poisonous Wastes Act 1972 and the Control of Pollution Act 1974). Details of bodies from which details can be obtained are given in the Bibliography.

Chain saw use also represents an area where hazards are great; the protective clothing required is:

1. Safety helmet (to BS 5240: 1975)
2. Ear defenders
3. Eye protection (goggles if used should be to BS 2092).
4. Gloves – ballistic nylon or kevlar protection for the back of the left hand
5. Leg protection – ballistic nylon or kevlar trousers, or
6. Safety boots – steel toecaps and ballistic nylon tongue
7. Non-snag high-visibility outer clothing.
8. First aid kit
9. Hand cleaning material.

In addition, ropes, harnesses, carabiners, etc. are required and full details are specified in Forestry Safety Council guides.

The safety clothing required for each operation should be carefully determined and its use enforced.

The choice needs to be governed by: the need of the user in terms of comfort and ease of movement, the scale and type of the hazard, any Regulations, specific job requirements and the cost of cleaning and maintenance, etc. The primary factor is user comfort and ease of use as any item which does not meet the criteria is certain to fail.

It is now realized that the health and safety of staff is not a fringe activity but one which occupies a major place in any organization and forms an integral part of working methods. If it is to play its full part in ensuring the success of an organization it requires commitment from each member of the workforce. Cooperation between professional advisers, managers and the man at the sharp end is essential if the objective of a safe working environment is to be achieved.

References

Amenity Pesticides 1988/89, British Agrochemicals Association

Code of Practice on the Use of Pesticides in Amenity Areas, National Turfgrass Council

Control of Pesticide Regulations 1986, HMSO

The Food and Environmental Protection Act 1985, HMSO

Forestry Safety Council, *Safety Guides FSC1–35; FSC N*

Guidelines for Applying Crop Protection Chemicals, HMSO Booklet B2272

Guidelines for the Disposal of Unwanted Pesticides on Farms and Holdings, HMSO Booklet B2198

Health and Safety at Work Act 1974, HMSO

Health and Safety Executive leaflets on *Training in the Use of Pesticides; Pesticides; Noise; Circular Saws; Safety with Chainsaws; Report that Accident; Lifting and Carrying; Prevention of Accidents; Writing a Safety Policy Statement – Advice to Employers*

Pesticides 1988 – Pesticides approved under the control of Pesticides Regulations 1986, HMSO Reference Book 500

Storage of Approved Pesticides: Guidance for Farmers and Other Professional Users, Health and Safety Executive Guidance Note CS 19

Straiks, Jeremy and Dewis, Malcolm (1986), *ROSPA Health and Safety Practice*, Pitman

UK Pesticide Guide, British Crop Protection Council

Chapter 7

MACHINERY AND EQUIPMENT

The Scale and Impact of Mechanization

For most types of landscape maintenance, machinery and transport is the next largest cost to wages, comprising 15–25 per cent of the total. It is therefore essential that the machinery is properly managed, not only to contain and control costs, but also to ensure that the right type of machinery is used and that it works reliably when it is needed. Poor equipment that is inadequate for the tasks, or unreliable or difficult to use, wastes valuable staff time but also causes frustration and annoyance and seriously depresses staff morale. Machinery therefore can be the key issue between an effective and efficient workforce or a demoralized disorganized rabble and false economies on equipment can quite easily increase overall costs.

Another fundamental effect of machinery is to alter the way in which landscapes are maintained and, in some circumstances, alter the design and appearance of that landscape to suit the needs of the equipment. As an example, large-capacity grass mowers generally need wide open spaces to operate effectively, and many small and intimate layouts have gradually been altered and simplified to make this possible. Conversely, the development of more efficient hedge-cutters has made hedges easier and cheaper to maintain and therefore helped to stem the trend of wholesale grubbing.

The effects of mechanization can be both positive and

detrimental and it is important that the landscape manager has clear objectives in arranging the regular maintenance and is not too easily diverted to cheap and easy mechanization where it is inappropriate.

The proper management of machinery and vehicles is a specialist task needing a detailed knowledge of various mechanical and legal implications. Any large maintenance organizations should therefore employ a suitably qualified manager with a specific responsibility for the machinery and vehicle fleet. If this fleet includes goods vehicles over 3.5 metric tonnes (gross weight) this manager is required by law to hold a Certificate of Competence as a transport manager issued by the Department of Transport and the organization will need to hold an Operators Licence ('O' Licence) also from the Department of Transport. For goods vehicles of 7.5 metric tonnes gross weight and over, the drivers will need to hold heavy goods vehicle driving licences.

Machinery Requirements and Capital Costs

The major equipment needs are mowers, of various types and sizes, various ancillary tools and, in nearly all cases, some form of transport for machinery, staff and materials. The exact requirements vary considerably according to the maintenance that is needed and, as shown in the examples below, the initial capital costs can vary from as little as £100 or so, to more than £3000 per hectare.

Example 1   *Country park or semi natural area of grass/woodland*

	Capital cost 1987 (excluding VAT)
	£
Pick up truck (4-wheel drive)	9,800
(or agricultural tractor*)	10,000
Trailer (for tractor or truck)	1,000
(Tractor-mounted flail or hay mower*)	1,300
Pedestrian-operated rotary mower say 600 mm cut	400
2 chain saws	700
Knapsack or similar sprayer	60
	Total £11,960 – 23,260

*Would not be required if contract hay cropping or grazing is adopted for any large grass area.

The above would probably be appropriate for the regular maintenance of sites of 50–100 hectares. While this might include occasional tree-felling it is assumed that most tree harvesting and timber extraction would be by separate contracts.

Example 2 *Recreation grounds, simple open spaces and verges in housing estates*

	Capital cost 1987
	£
Tractor (approximately 40 b.h.p.)	10,000
Tractor trailer	1,000
Five-unit gang mower and carrier	10,000
'Ride-on' triple mower	3,000
Pedestrian-operated rotary mower or flymo, say 500 mm cut	350
2 mechanical strimmers	600
Knapsack or similar sprayer	60
	Total £25,010

Appropriate for two people maintaining up to about 50 hectares of open space.

Example 3 *Housing estates with small open spaces and formal amenity areas with planted borders*

	Capital cost 1987
	£
Pick-up truck or van	6,800
Trailer	1,000
'Ride-on' triple mower	3,000
Pedestrian-operated cylinder mower (say 600 mm cut)	900
Pedestrian-operated rotary mower (500 mm cut)	350
2 petrol-driven hedge trimmers	500
2 mechanical strimmers	600
2 knapsack sprayers or similar	100
	Total £13,250

Appropriate for two people maintaining up to 10 hectares of mixed open space and planted areas, or a large formal garden (hand truck instead of the pick-up truck and trailer).

Example 4   *Small areas of building surrounds, gardens or similar formal areas*

	Capital cost 1987
	£
Pick-up truck or van	6,800
Trailer	1,000
2 pedestrian-operated mowers (say 600 mm cut)	1,800
Pedestrian-operated rotary mower (500 mm cut)	500
2 petrol-driven hedge trimmers	500
2 knapsack sprayers or similar	100
	Total £10,700

Appropriate for two people maintaining a number of small sites up to a total area of approximately 5 hectares.

Example 5   *Sports grounds and playing fields*

	Capital cost 1987
	£
Tractor (approximately 40 bhp)	10,000
Trailer (preferably tipping)	1,000
5 unit gang-mower and carrier	10,000
Large pedestrian-operated cylinder mower (900 mm cut)	2,300
Small pedestrian-operated cylinder mower (400 mm cut)	700
Rotary mower or flymo (500 mm cut)	350
Tractor-mounted spiker	600
Tractor-mounted harrows	250
Tractor-mounted gang roller	1,600
Tractor-mounted fertilizer spreader	400
Tractor-mounted sprayer	1,000
Tractor-mounted contravator	4,700
Self-propelled motor roller	10,000
Pedestrian-operated spiker/scarifyer	1,200
Knapsack sprayer	60
	Total £44,160

Appropriate for up to 40 hectares of well-used playing fields including fine turf areas such as cricket squares and hockey pitches. Some equipment (e.g. sprayers) could be shared over a larger area but more pedestrian mowers and rollers may be required to cope with a high proportion of fine turf.

In all the examples the machinery and transport needs have been set at a reasonable minimum but do not account for any savings that might be made by occasional hiring or sharing between different groups of staff. Neither, however, do they account for any extras that may be needed to act as reserves in peak work times or in the event of breakdowns. (See later section.)

The Choice of Equipment

In the United Kingdom we are fortunate in having a wide range of maintenance equipment available, so much so that the choice can often be bewildering. Another characteristic of the machinery market is that there are a number of relatively small firms with limited resources who are only able to carry out a minimum of design and development work before marketing new and revamped models. This last fact emphasizes the advantage of purchasing from the larger experienced manufacturers as well as the need for careful choice of any new equipment. The following factors are important.

Price:In a competitive market it is generally true that you get what you pay for. Therefore, as a general rule, the more expensive machines are better engineered and robust and built to sustain more continual and heavy use and have a longer economic life. Thus, unless light and infrequent use is expected, it can be a very false economy to purchase cheaper machines, designed for mainly domestic use, for the more robust professional models.

Undesirable features in professional machines include:

- light metal framings and mountings, friction or sometimes

belt-driven instead of chain or gear mechanisms, simple journal bearing or bushes in place of roller bearings
- low-life engines usually with simple cast cylinders and journal bearings
- unnecessary decorative cowlings that may restrict air cooling and servicing
- relatively poor provision for operator comfort.

Area or volume of work: Larger, high-capacity machines can usually only be justified if there is a need to work them at or near their full capacity. In the case of mowing machines this is very important (see later section) and the machines must be matched to the areas of work involved.

In this respect, manufacturer's performance figures should be treated with some caution as they are usually quoted for the actual operating time on site. Time must also be allowed for:

Transporting to and from site
Regular servicing, starting up, adjustments and putting away
Downtime through breakdowns or accidents
Lost time through wet weather
Regular interruptions to the work, e.g. clearing or mowing around obstructions.

All these factors tend significantly to reduce the performance from the ideal potential. Also the use that can be made of a machine will depend on how much work can be made available to it without excessive and uneconomic transporting it from site to site.

On site access and manoeuvrability: Machine sizes must allow access through gates and openings on site and be able to pass between and around trees, posts and other obstacles. The following are important:

Overall transport width, including for road travel and transport on trailers. 2.5 m is the usual maximum
Turning circle. Rear-wheel steering is more effective
Ground clearance for mowing up or over kerbs and other changes in level
Overall weight for transport and/or lifting
Wheel ground weight for soil compaction and possible

marking of turf and damage to hard paving and manhole covers.

Ease of adjustments and servicing: Height adjustments and the like should be easy and positive, as should access to regular servicing points, grease nipples, oilplugs, etc. Regular servicing and adjustment is often neglected by many staff and this will be encouraged if the operations are difficult.

Noise, comfort and safety: The Health and Safety at Work Act 1974 and consumer law now puts a firm obligation on the manufacturers to ensure that machines are fit for their purpose and safe, both for the operator and public at large. This, among other things, means the provision of adequate guards for moving parts and arrangements to prevent contact of feet and fingers with cutting cylinders and flails. In some cases these safety fixtures can inhibit the most effective operation of the machines and its servicing and adjustment if they are not skilfully designed.

Less obvious dangers for long-term users are the effects of noise and vibration. Even quite moderate noise levels, over a long period of time, can gradually cause partial deafness, and loud engine noise will often cause the operator to work the machine at a lower speed below its optimum. Small engines, e.g. on chain saws, are a particular problem as heavy muffling of the exhaust can seriously reduce the power-to-weight ratio. Operators must therefore be provided with ear protection for these machines but ear muffs should preferably be used for any machine where the engine noise causes discomfort.

Machinery or engine noise is usually measured in decibels (dB) on a logarithmic scale that represents the pressure of the sound waves. A refinement of this system is to adjust the reading to take account of the effect of different frequencies on the human ear and this is represented by the symbols dB(A). On this scale, most people will *perceive* a doubling of a noise level for every increase of 10 points but, in fact, because of the logarithmic nature of the reading, the noise, and its damaging effect, is doubled for every three points.

Above 100 dB(A) the noise will cause considerable discomfort for even short periods and hearing damage if it is continued for any length of time. Between 80 and 100 dB(A) a noise is less likely to cause immediate discomfort but will cause hearing damage over a period of time.

A safe working limit for an eight-hour day is currently recognized as being 90 dB(A) but medical opinion on this is divided and lower levels should probably be aimed for. Noise levels above 90 dB(A) must therefore restrict the working day as below:

Noise level dB(A)	*Safe working time* (hours)
90	8
93	4
96	2
99	1
102	$\frac{1}{2}$

Tests carried out by the Kent County Council in 1981 on a range of mowing equipment and a chain saw, recorded the following noise levels as they would be perceived by the operator's ear:

Machine	*Noise level dB(A)*
Small cylinder mowers	82–9 (older machines tended to be noisier)
Tractor mounted hydraulic gang-mower	92 (90 with the cab windows shut)
Chain saw	110

Various types of ear defenders, muffs, plugs, etc. will protect an operator's hearing against damage and, for instance, a well-fitted pair of ear muffs should reduce the received noise level by at least 25 decibels. However, these devices are uncomfortable to wear for long periods and the long-term aim should be to try to reduce the source of the noise by, for instance, better muffling of engine exhausts and proper adjustment of moving parts. New agricultural tractors are now required to be fitted with quiet cabs (Q cabs) which restrict the noise levels to 90 dB(A). However, these noise levels are likely to be exceeded if the windows are opened. As this is a common practice in fine weather, the driver should be supplied with and required to wear ear muffs or similar protection when the need arises.

Ear muffs must be worn when using a chain saw as even quite short spells of operation produce damaging noise levels.

Under government regulations, the Lawnmowers (Harmonization of Noise Emissions Standards) Regulations 1986, implemented from July 1987, all new rotary mowers must have noise levels with certain limits as shown below:

Mower cutting width	*Maximum permitted sound level*
up to 50 cm	69 dB(A)
51–120 cm	100 dB(A)
over 120 cm	105 dB(A)

Similar regulations are forecast for cylinder mowers, probably coming into effect in 1990 but, in the meantime, even these new design noise levels for rotary mowers mean that anyone using a medium to large rotary mower for even an hour or so, should wear efficient ear protectors.

In addition to the effects of noise, engine vibrations transmitted through machine handles can cause 'white fingers' by affecting the blood flow and nervous system. In serious cases, the condition can become permanent. Such problems have largely been overcome on chain saws by anti-vibration mountings, or the use of padded gloves, but slight symptoms can be caused on any small engine machine that is used for a long period of time.

Lower frequency vibrations through the seats of agricultural tractors have been shown to cause back injuries over a long period of time, but tractors are now fitted with anti-vibration seats which are safer and more comfortable. It is unlikely that these injuries would result from the relatively short-term use of small ride-on mowers or garden tractors but the seats should be made as comfortable as possible with adequate springing.

Operator's preference: After price and operating effectiveness, this is probably one of the most important factors in the final choice of a piece of equipment. Nearly all machinery needs sympathetic care and adjustment if it is to give good service and this is only likely to be forthcoming if the operator perceives a machine as being a good one. It is therefore important to involve the user in selection of the machinery and if at all possible have the casting vote in the final decision.

In practice, this can be very difficult and, at the extreme, lead to a wide range of different machines for doing the same job. Consequent difficulties are the need to hold larger stocks of spares and the repairs themselves may take longer because fitters are relatively unfamiliar with particular machines. It is therefore advisable to have a consistent buying policy formed out of consultation with the operators and updated on the basis of their experience of particular types of machines.

Selection of Mowing Equipment

In England grassland forms the major framework of the landscape and mowing is probably the single most important mechanical task, often representing as much as 60 per cent of the annual workload. Matching the mowers to the task in hand is essential both to make the best use of capital but also to ensure this basic operation is carried out effectively so that the other work can be built on a sound base.

There are three main methods of mowing: the cylinder or reel cutter, the rotary or flail mower, and the reciprocating blade cutter.

The cylinder mower is the system most commonly used for fine to medium turf and is the only method that will produce the smooth finish demanded for many sports surfaces and amenity lawns. It is relatively fast and energy-efficient but will not cope adequately with long grass and needs careful adjustment and use to keep it working well.

The rotary flail mowers are much more robust and are able to cope with both long and short grass in relatively inexperienced hands. They are, however, rather slower in operation and less energy-efficient. They are also potentially more dangerous to use because of the high-speed revolving blades. Mowers with the blades revolving in a horizontal plane are normally best for short to medium-length grass, but the flail mower, with blades revolving in a vertical plane, are able to deal with much coarser vegetation. Thus they are particularly suitable for rural road verges and other areas that are only mown once or a few times a year.

The reciprocating blade principle, based on the traditional hay cutter, has relatively little use in amenity horticulture although it is still well used in agriculture, e.g. combine harvesters. The cutting blades need fairly frequent sharpening and are easily damaged by hitting concealed objects. None the less, these mowers can be very effective in mowing tall-standing grass, provided it is not flattened or matted.

The basic choice between the different mowing methods is governed by the frequency of cutting. Turf that is mown at least every ten days at the height of the growing season will almost certainly be best mown with a cylinder mower. At longer mowing intervals the cylinder mower will have increasing difficulty with coping with the mass of the grass growth and rotary mowers, though generally slower in operation, are more suitable. At very low mowing frequencies, four cuts or fewer per year, the rotary mowers will also have difficulty with the volume of vegetation and flails are more effective.

Within each category of mowing, there is a wide range of small and large mowers that can be used but, in relative costs, the bigger the machine the lower the cost of mowing per area. This is illustrated in Figure 7.1 which shows the costs per hour and per hectare of using a large and small cylinder mower.

Choice of Machine in Relation to Area

Unfortunately, from a cost point of view, the use of the large machines is often restricted by the simple constraints of space and the layout of the sites. This means that the capital cost of the larger mower can only usually be justified where there is a need to mow large areas of grass, and the actual cost of mowing will depend on the utilization of the mower in relation to its potential capacity.

In order to evaluate this, it is convenient to assume that there are two main elements in the annual costs of operating a machine.

(a) The 'standing charges'. These are capital charges and depreciation which will vary to some extent on the use of the machine but, within broad limits, the life and capital

	600 mm pedestrian machine	Tractor mounted 7 unit powered gang-mower
Wages, etc.	5.00	5.00
Fuel	0.25	1.50
Repairs and servicing	0.25	2.85
Depreciation and interest charges	0.30	4.30
	£5.80	£13.65
	Based on 400 hours use per year	Based on 700 hours use per year
Approximate area cut per hour (excluding travelling, etc.).	1,500 m²	2.25 hectares
Cost per hectare of mowing	£39	£6

Figure 7.1 *The costs of an hour's mowing using cylinder machines (1986 prices)*

depreciation will be determined by the design and construction of the machine. Thus the 'standing charges' per year can be calculated as depreciation plus interest on capital, i.e.

$$\frac{\text{capital cost} - \text{resale value}}{\text{machine life in years}} +$$

$$\frac{(\text{capital cost} - \text{resale value}) \times \% \text{ interest rate}}{2}$$

The interest charge is based on the assumption of a straight-line depreciation so that average capital employed in any one year is half the capital cost less the final resale value.

(b) The variable costs directly related to the hours of use, wages, fuel, repairs and servicing.

By combining these costs as shown in Table 7.1, it is possible to compare the likely annual costs of mowing varying areas of grass with different sizes of machine. This theoretical analysis

Table 7.1 *Mowing costs in relation to the area of mowing* (1986 figures)

Machine (capital cost)	Annual charge (depr. & int.)	Hourly charge (labour, repairs, etc.)	Hours to mow a hectare (2)	Annual cost of mowing of given areas (20 times per year)								
				$\frac{1}{2}$	1	2	3	5	10	15	20	30
Pedestrian mowers .6 m cut .75 cm (£860)	£120	£5.50	6.7	£490	£860	£1,590						
(£2,800)	£390	£6.30	5.0	£750	£1,020	£1,650	£2,280					
'Ride-on' triple 1.8 cm cut (£3,800)	£650	£7.00	2.5 to		£1,000	£1,350	£1,700	£2,400	£4,150	£5,900		
			1.5		£860	£1,070	£1,280	£1,700	£2,750	£3,800	£4,850	
Tractor gang-mower 4.65 m cut (£21,500 inc. tractor)	£3,000	£9.35	0.45						£3,840	£4,260	£4,680	£5,520

1. Based on eight years' life and 5 per cent interest for all except the 'Ride on' triple which has an assumed six years' life.
2. Estimates based on work study times but excluding any travelling costs, servicing time, etc.

147

will not, of course, apply in all circumstances. The rates of mowing will vary according to the detail of the layout and motivation of the operators. Capital charges will depend on the source of finance but 5 per cent has been chosen as that currently set by government regulations as the required return on capital employed by Direct Labour Organizations.

On the basis of Table 7.1 it is likely that the 'ride-on' triple mower becomes an economic proposition for quite small areas (2 hectares or less), even if the layout is complicated. Therefore for straightforward and simple layouts, and a higher rate of mowing, the triple mower could be economic at even one hectare of turf, i.e. only used for about two hours per week.

As an alternative, the large pedestrian-operated mower does not appear to justify its capital cost and would therefore only be used if there was a special need to provide a large area of fine smooth turf, e.g. for hockey pitches or a 'quality' cricket outfield.

At the other end of the scale, the very high-capacity tractor-mounted gang-mower only comes into its own at about 15–20 hectares and this confirms the value of the cheaper triple mower for medium areas of turf.

In addition to the actual mowing times allowed in Table 7.2, it is necessary to take account of any travelling between sites which will, in effect, increase the net time taken to mow a particular area. These factors have to be estimated for each set of circumstances but, by adopting a disciplined approach as outlined above, it will be possible to evaluate the economic consequences of different machinery options.

Economic Machine Lives and Replacement Policies

When a machine or vehicle is kept in operation for a long time the capital costs are spread over a longer base and the depreciation per month or year of use is reduced. However, as the machine becomes older, the costs of servicing and repair tend to increase. This relationship is represented in general form in Figure 7.2 which indicates that the total cost per year (depreciation and repairs) will usually fall in the early years but

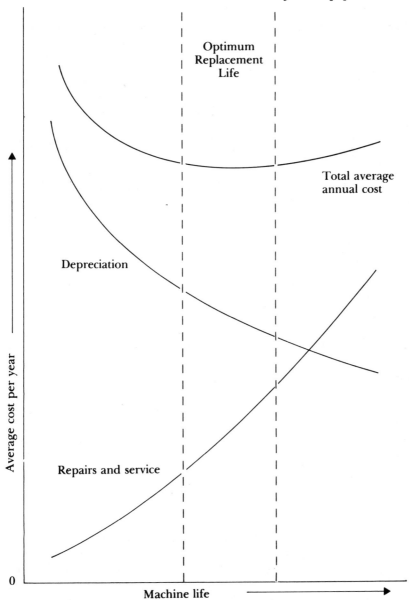

Figure 7.2 *Typical relationship of machinery depreciation and maintenance costs*

Table 7.2 *Depreciation and repair costs for gangmowing tractors based on age*

Age in years	Estimated resale value	Total depreciation	Repair and servicing		Life total costs	Average annual costs
			For the year	Life total		
1	7,000	3,000	100	100	3,100	3,100
2	5,250	4,750	510	610	5,360	2,680
3	4,200	5,800	333	940	6,740	2,247
4	3,360	6,640	590	1,530	8,170	2,042
5	2,680	7,320	830	2,360	9,680	1,936
6	2,140	7,860	520	2,880	10,740	1,790
7	1,700	8,300	950	3,830	12,130	1,732
8	1,400	8,600	900	4,730	13,330	1,666
9	1,100	8,900	1,530	6,260	15,160	1,684
10	900	9,100	550	6,810	15,910	1,591

then increase again as the equipment becomes more expensive to maintain.

Although this basic pattern applies to most types of vehicle and mechanical equipment, the details vary considerably according to the type of equipment and its construction. Thus light machine tools, like chain saws, will have relatively rapid depreciation and high repair costs after a short time. Conversely, a well-built motor roller can be kept for many years with very low annual depreciation and stable repair costs. An example from a fleet of around 50 agricultural tractors, mainly used for gang-mowing, is shown in Table 7.2. The figures in the table were calculated by averaging the repair costs in one year (1987) for each age group of tractors. The number of tractors in each age group was not exactly the same and so it would be wrong to put too much emphasis on any one year's figures, but they do show the general trend that is likely to occur.

In this particular example, the annual average costs do not appear to rise significantly however long the tractor is kept, although the cost of repairs can be very high. However, this table does not include the inconvenience and management problems that arise from having an elderly machine that is more likely to break down in the peak of the season. Such costs are difficult to quantify, as are the advantages of the psychological motivation that the driver might receive from having a new tractor at more frequent intervals, and a machine that is more up to date in design and improvement.

Taking these considerations into account it would be worthwhile replacing the tractors as soon as the major reductions in annual average costs have taken place. Thus in the example in Table 7.2, the minimum average annual cost is reached after 8–10 years, but the average costs fall relatively slowly after about six years. Thus, taking the other factors into account, it may be more economic, in overall terms, to replace the tractors at between six and eight years. In practice, this would probably mean having a basic replacement life of six years, but then retaining those that are in better than average condition, for up to a further two years on the basis of an engineer's annual inspection and estimation of likely repair and servicing costs.

In order that these considerations can be properly evaluated, it is essential to have a system of recording the costs of repairs and servicing against each item of plant so that the average trends in depreciation and running costs can be established. This basic information can then be used to estimate the likely economic life as indicated in Table 7.2. The economic life will vary from organization to organization according to the intensity and type of use, as well as the servicing levels, but it can also be significantly influenced by any bulk purchase discounts that the owner is able to negotiate on the new equipment. Thus, particularly in the case of vehicles, a discount on the initial purchase price will reduce the depreciation in the early years and therefore make a relatively quick resale advantageous.

All these various factors need to be evaluated by each employer but the list overleaf shows some typical replacement lives for a range of common items.

Once a list of replacement lives has been established, it is administratively convenient to adopt it as a standard and make regular arrangements to replace equipment as it reaches the specified age. Capital finance can also be accurately forecast, and repairs and overhauls geared to take account of predicted sales. However, in practice not all machines will wear at the same rate and it is often advantageous to replace some machines earlier than the average to avoid major repairs or overhauls. Conversely, some items will be in good condition as they approach their replacement time and can be kept for longer, either in active service or as a reserve to be used in the event of breakdowns.

Small cylinder mower	7 – 10 years
Small rotary mower	3 – 5 years
Flymower	2 – 5 years
Chain saw	2 – 5 years
Petrol-driven hedge-cutter	2 – 5 years
Ride-on triple mower	4 – 7 years
Agricultural tractor	7 – 10 years
Pick-up truck or transit van	4 – 7 years
Lorry	5 – 8 years

Renewal Funds

For any rational replacement policy it is essential to have the necessary capital available so that the new equipment can be purchased at the optimum time. However, the demand of this capital is likely to vary considerably from year to year depending on which items of equipment become due for replacement. In general, therefore, the money either has to be borrowed or taken from other reserves, or even funds for other projects. Not surprisingly, there is often some reluctance to release the capital when it is needed but the potential difficulties of this can often be overcome by setting up a special renewals fund.

In essence this means that regular sums are set aside each year to meet the cost of future purchases and the money is invested until it is needed. Annual payments to the fund are calculated to meet the average cost of purchases over the next five to ten years, assuming that the machines are replaced in accordance with the economic replacement lives established from past experience (see Table 7.3 for a simplified example). By setting up a replacement fund, a manager imposes the discipline of planning the overall capital requirements but also ensures that the regular costs of machinery depreciation are

Table 7.3 *Example of machinery renewals fund calculation*

Item	No. in fleet	Current replacement cost	Replacement life years	Capital requirements and (number to be replaced)				
				Year 1	Year 2	Year 3	Year 4	Year 5
Small cylinder mowers	20	700	8	(2) 1,400	(4) 2,800	(3) 2,100	(5) 3,500	(1) 700
Small rotary mowers	16	350	4	(5) 1,750	(2) 700	(4) 1,400	(5) 1,750	(5) 1,750
'Ride-on' triple mowers	5	3,000	5	(1) 3,000	—	(2) 6,000	(2) 6,000	—
Gang-mower tractors	4	10,000	8	—	—	(2) 20,000	(1) 20,000	—
Gang-mowers and trailer	3	10,000	8	—	—	(2) 20,000	(1) 20,000	—
Team van	8	6,800	6	(1) 6,800	(2) 13,600	(2) 13,600	(1) 6,800	(1) 6,800
Total per year				12,950	17,100	63,100	58,050	9,250

5-year total   £160,450

Average annual contribution   £32,090

Note

The annual contributions may need to be varied to account for:
increases in the price of machinery and the interest earned on the fund
the resale value of the replaced machinery and vehicles.

properly met on a year to year basis and, at least in accounting terms, the organization is not living on its capital.

Leasing and Hire Arrangements

The capital for machinery and vehicles is a significant cost on any organization, and there is an obvious need to keep the stock of capital equipment, and premises and other property, to an economic minimum. In local government Direct Work Organizations, this need has been emphasized by the compulsory competition legislation (Local Government Act 1988) which uses return on capital employed as the main criterion for testing financial viability.

As an alternative to owning equipment there are various leasing arrangements which avoid the need for large capital outlay, but not the interest charges. These arrangements can vary from purely financial schemes which merely supply capital needed for purchase, to other long-term leases which include servicing and even back-up replacements in the event of breakdowns or failure. Under the government competition legislation, Direct Works Organizations will not avoid the need to make a return on the capital value of leased equipment and, in capital accounting terms, leased equipment is regarded as owned. Equipment that is hired on hourly or daily charges, with or without the operator, is not counted as owned and so decisions on hiring specialist equipment can be based on the simple comparison of likely annual hire charges compared with the costs of ownership (including return on capital, depreciation, servicing and repairs, etc.).

Servicing and Overhaul Policies

As a very broad generalization, the cost of servicing and repairs of an item of grounds maintenance equipment is likely to be of the order of the cost of its capital depreciation. Thus, for instance if a £1000 mower has an economic life of five years, the average cost of servicing and repairs will probably be of the order of £200 a year. There are considerable variations around this rule but, as a guideline, it indicates the general order of costs that are likely to arise.

To a significant extent the variations will depend on the servicing and repair policy that is adopted and, at the extreme, there are two distinct strategies; programmed maintenance and breakdown maintenance.

Programmed maintenance is the system that, we hope, airlines will adopt. The various mechanical and structural parts of an aircraft have a defined serviceable life and at pre-planned times the vital parts are stripped down and inspected and/or replaced. Similar procedures, and for similar reasons, are often adopted for machines like gang-mowers and, at the end of the mowing season, they are often stripped down and overhauled so that the chances of breakdowns in the middle of the mowing season are kept to a minimum.

Breakdown maintenance would appear to be less responsible in that the machine is merely run until it fails and at that stage, it is repaired. For some cheaper items, and depending on the failures, the broken machine will merely be thrown away and replaced with a new one. For example, small rotary mowers are rarely worth repairing once the main engine bearings have failed and it may be appropriate to adopt a policy of buying small cheap machines with the intention of throwing them away when they start to fail (and keeping a few new ones in stock against the eventual failure).

For bigger and more expensive machines the event of a mechanical breakdown can have more serious consequences but the regular overhaul at the end of each season can be an expensive luxury, and lead to the replacement of components before the end of their working life. (Once a machine is stripped down it is very tempting, and probably sensible, to replace parts that are even slightly worn.) Overhauling at the end of every other season, for instance, may be sufficient, and only slightly increase mid-season breakdowns.

In practice, the right compromise between programmed and breakdown maintenance has to be arrived at for each organization and as a reflection of the work it undertakes, and the type of machinery it uses.

Reserve Equipment

Whatever the policy of overhaul and servicing it is inevitable
that some machines will become unserviceable at sometime in
the season, either through mechanical breakdown or more
frequently through misuse or accidents (e.g. mowing cylinders
smashed on hidden items). At worst, even the loss of a day's
mowing can seriously disrupt the work programme, particularly if manning and machinery levels have been closely
matched to the workload. It is therefore important to have
some reserve machines available or other arrangements that
will deal with this eventuality.

The level of machinery reserves is principally a matter for
commercial judgement, assessing the risks involved and the
effectiveness of repair arrangements. Thus, the need for
reserves is much reduced if the consequences of delay through
breakdown are small and/or the repair facilities are swift and
effective. In general, the consequences of delay are most likely
to be significant for formal landscapes or for sports grounds
where, for instance, the playing surfaces might quickly become
unsatisfactory. In these types of situations around a 10 per cent
reserve of critical items has usually been found necessary to
provide a reasonable continuity of service. This level of reserve
can be provided with a large organization by holding stocks of
say:

- replacement cutting units for gang-mowers
- reserve engines for common mowers
- machines that are still serviceable but past their replacement
  life.

For a smaller organization, the holding of these stocks would be
relatively more expensive and more reliance would need to be
placed on the built-in reserve that comes from using a range of
equipment. For instance, a small rotary mower, mainly used for
cutting rough grass, can be used as a back-up for small cylinder
mowers on most lawns, even though they might be slower and
give a less attractive finish. The overall need is therefore slightly
to over-provide with equipment so that work programmes can
be reasonably maintained throughout the average season.

Chapter 8

BUDGET AND COST CONTROL

Annual Budgets

An annual budget is probably the essential first step in any system of financial control and management. The process of the preparation of the budget focuses attention on a number of important issues including:

the overall level of finance available

the allocation of the total to the main items of expenditure, e.g. wages, machinery, etc.

the sub-allocation of resources to specific projects or, in the case of large organizations, to area managers

the necessary framework for cost control and monitoring throughout the year

the expected levels of income, for trading organizations, and therefore the cost ceilings necessary for desired profit levels

the capital requirements, for machinery, etc.

anticipated inflation of wage and other costs.

In large organizations like local authorities, the process of preparing an annual budget is an extremely complicated one and the landscape manager can often find himself severely constrained by the demands of the Treasurer's Department and the democratic processes of fixing policy options and the annual rate demand. Thus it is not unusual for the exact content of the budget still to be undetermined at the start of the financial year or even later, and the process of fixing a grounds maintenance budget is often one of evolution, rather than *ad hoc* decision-making. In these circumstances the manager often has to make a series of estimates about likely income and expenditure in order to plan ahead for the appointment of staff and purchase of materials and machinery. In this respect the commonly used financial year of April to March is not very helpful as most of the important planning decisions about staff numbers and orders for machinery have to be made at least three months before the start of the main growing season.

In a landscape contracting business the manager has greater control over the budget-making process and can choose the most suitable financial year end, but there is often a much greater uncertainty about likely income.

Table 8.1 is an example of the annual budget for an 'in-house' contractor for a local authority and shows the main budget headings that are commonly used.

In arriving at the budget figures a major consideration is the out-turn figure for the previous year. However, as the budget is usually being produced before the previous year is ended, the out-turn figures are only available for part of the year. This means that the only reliable figures for a full year out-turn are two years behind the new budget year. This makes the estimation of inflationary costs rather more difficult and wherever possible the budget figure should be worked back 'from base' at the current costs, e.g. the proposed number of staff × current wage rates and on costs.

The order of estimation is first to establish the likely income from various sources and then decide on wage and other allocations to match the total income.

Wages and machinery represent the major part of the budget costs and therefore demand the most scrutiny. It is therefore important to make a detailed analysis of the staff numbers each year, taking into account likely changes in workload and the labour-saving machinery, or otherwise, that is going to be available. Thus, for instance, the purchase of a 'ride-on' triple mower may well enable a staff reduction or, for instance, the 'mobilization' of two or more staff who were previously working alone on separate sites.

Staffing levels can also be influenced by decisions to contract

Table 8.1   *Example of a grounds maintenance budget*

Grounds maintenance budget 1987/88

Expenditure		£	%
Employees including area managers and foremen			
Wages and salaries, etc.		2,472,500	
Training		21,700	
Allowances		25,300	
	Sub-total	2,519,500	63.0
Premises and depots			
Maintenance and improvements		36,600	
Services		21,400	
Furniture and fittings		5,500	
Rent and rates		31,200	
Loan charges		12,000	
	Sub-total	106,700	2.7
Supplies and services			
Equipment		2,500	
Consumable materials		325,500	
Protective clothing		12,000	
Contract services/fees		115,000	
	Sub-total	455,000	11.4
Transport and machinery			
Running costs		400,000	
Renewals Fund contributions		260,000	
Additional machinery		20,000	
	Sub-total	680,000	17.0
General office/depot expenses			
Head office staff		220,700	
Telephones, post advertising, etc.		18,100	
	Sub-total	238,800	6.0
	Total	4,000,000	

out various specialist tasks or whole areas of work where it is
more economic to do so.

For machinery costs the purchase of replacement equipment
can vary considerably from year to year and sometimes be
constrained by the need to keep within a fixed budget. These
difficulties can be largely overcome by the provision of

relatively fixed payments to a renewals fund or by equipment leasing (see Chapter 7).

Calculation of Charges

Any trading organization has to decide on the charges (or tenders) it will make to its clients for the services that are provided. Charges must not be confused with costs which are the actual expenditure incurred by the organization in providing the service.

For an 'in-house' contractor in, for instance, a local authority or in a large industrial concern, the aim will usually be to make the charges (the income) to match or break even with the costs (expenditure), including the financing of the capital requirements. For a commercial contractor the charges will need to cover the cost plus the profit due to the shareholders or owners of the business. Similar demands may also be made of 'in-house' contractors by requiring them to make a specified percentage return or profit on capital employed or turnover and such conditions have been included in the legislation on compulsory competition.

In landscape work it is usual to express the charges in terms of cost per hour of work so that these hourly rates can be used for preparing tender prices or accounts for work carried out on day work rates. In their simplest form they can be calculated thus:

$$\text{Charge per hour} = \frac{\text{Total cost of the organization}}{\text{Total number of productive hours of work}}$$

This simple calculation would give an average rate for a wide range of work and so in many situations the actual costs would vary quite widely from the charges, i.e. the cheaper operations would subsidize the work that requires expensive machinery or materials.

In order to make the charges more representative of the costs it is usual to allocate to a number of subheadings and calculate separate hourly charges. At the extreme these hourly charges

Table 8.2 *Example of detailed hourly charges*

Item	Charge rate
Gardener labourer	5.30 per hour
Semi-skilled gardener	5.70 per hour
Skilled gardener	6.10 per hour
Supervision cost	1.60 per man-hour
Use of hand tools	.20 per man-hour
Provision of transport to and from site	.50 per man-hour
Small motor mower up to 600 mm cut (cylinder or rotary)	.40 per hour
Large motor mower up to 1.2 m cut (cylinder or rotary)	.80 per hour
Hand-held hedge trimmer or chain saw, petrol driven	.50 per hour

can extend to even the use of individual pieces of quite small equipment as shown in Table 8.2.

Using a range of hourly charges such as those indicated above it is possible to arrive at composite charges for almost any maintenance operation which, in general, should be a fair representation of the likely costs. However, the calculation of the individual charges relies on estimates of the likely hours of use of, say, particular types of machine, and it is time-consuming and often difficult to monitor these estimates against the actual use. The task can be eased by adopting charges per day rather than per hour, but for most purposes the charges can be consolidated into a relatively few charge rates. For example the minimum might be:

1. Mobile grounds staff rate per hour, i.e. including cost of transport of machinery and manpower up to and including small 'ride-on' mowers (transported by trailer), and 'day-to-day' materials and all supervision.
2. On-site grounds staff rate per hour. As above but excluding cost of transport.
3. Tractor and driver rate using simple cultivation equipment or trailer.
4. Tractor and driver rate using trailed or power-driven gang-mower.
5. Lorry and driver rate per hour for collection and delivery of bulk materials.

6. Labour only rate for transport and attendance on site for manual operations only using hand tools (e.g. suitable for snow-clearing and tree-planting).

The exact details and ranges of the hire rates will vary from organization to organization and be developed to suit their own particular needs. However, with large organizations there is a need to decide on the size of the working unit or 'cost centre' for which the rate is calculated. For instance, if there is a number of relatively separate area depots or managers, the productivity in the use of labour and machinery may vary considerably. If a single cost centre is adopted, i.e. the costs are calculated on the overall average, the efficient areas will be burdened with the relatively high costs of the less efficient. This may mean that the less efficient may just be able to stay competitive, but also that the efficient will not be able to compete as well as they might. It is therefore preferable to establish cost centres which match as closely as possible with the separate working units, an arrangement that is now practicable through the use of computer accounting systems. For example, a unit covered by a first line supervisor or area foreman would be ideal covering from as few as 5 up to 15 or so staff. In particular, the knowledge amongst a group of this size that their performance is reflected in their cost-competitive ability is a powerful motivator to both the supervisor and staff.

Seasonal Variation of Charges

Although it is usual to calculate charges for a whole year there are circumstances where the manager may wish to vary the rates to:

- accommodate aggressive tendering, i.e. to tender on zero profit or loss-making rates to keep staff employed when work is scarce
- reflect the high costs of *ad hoc* 'high season' tasks that do not provide continuity of employment
- take advantage of high market rates when there are temporary, or longer, manpower shortages.

All these are matters for commercial judgement but it is important that these judgements are made on the basis of the actual costs compared with the charges made and therefore the respective subsidies or extra profits that they represent.

Estimation of Productive Man-hours

Although the overall cost of wages, machinery, etc. are relatively easy to estimate, the number of productive hours can be more difficult as it has to take account of the following:

Losses through	*Possible quantities*
Annual leave	8 per cent or more
Bank holidays	
Union meetings	1 – 2 per cent
Training	
Sickness/injury	2 – 5 per cent
Wet time	5 per cent
Other lost time, breakdowns, etc.	5 per cent
Staff vacancies	5 per cent
Time spent on	
Machinery servicing and maintenance	5 per cent
Travelling from depot to sites	up to 25 per cent (but might be included in the charges)
Gains from	
Overtime	5 per cent
Working supervisors and casual staff	5 per cent

The actual incidence of these losses, and gains, from the total working year can be ascertained from time-sheets and will probably vary considerably from cost centre to cost centre and have a significant effect on the actual costs.

In a typical case a worker employed on the basis of 39 hours a week throughout the year would have a potential of $52 \times 39 =$

2028 work-hours per year. After allowing for the losses and gains listed above the actual productive hours, including travelling between sites and daily preparation times, are only likely to be around 70 per cent of the potential or around 1400 hours per year.

Thus, in the example shown in Table 8.1, if there were 270 operatives employed, the overall hourly charge rate would be:

$$\frac{£4,000,000}{270 \times 1,400} = £10.8$$

On the assumption that the staff are paid an average of £7000 per year (or £140 per week), the charge rate of £10.56 is approximately three times the hourly wage rate paid to the staff, i.e.

$$\frac{£7,000 \text{ per year}}{2,028 \text{ hours/year}} = £3.45 \text{ per hour}$$

Alternatively this means that the on costs on wages paid are likely to be of the order of 200 per cent.

Cost Control

For the owner of a private estate, or for the maintenance of a single sports field complex, the grounds maintenance cost control can be fairly straightforward. Provided the budget has been properly prepared, and staff and machinery levels set accordingly, there are likely to be few major changes in costs, except perhaps for major breakdowns in machinery. It is therefore sufficient to monitor the total costs against budget at approximately three-monthly intervals with a more detailed look after the main growing season to plan any special winter projects or machinery repairs.

Larger organizations will also keep relatively close to forecast costs if the budget has been properly prepared but, for a trading organization, the costs of providing a specified level of service can vary considerably because of weather patterns or gradual changes in the staff productivity. It is therefore important to monitor the costs regularly, say at monthly intervals, in order to try to rectify any undesirable trends before they become too serious.

With computer-based accounting systems, these frequent reviews can be carried out at relatively little extra cost, provided the input data is as up to date as possible. In most systems the costs or income are only actually taken into account when either the bill has been presented and paid or the income has actually been received. This usually means that there is a significant lag in the figures for outside suppliers, e.g. for materials or machinery repairs, but the figures for wages, the major cost, are likely to be much more up to date. These influences need to be kept in mind when reviewing the data but the following comparisons are probably the most valuable indicators:

total income received against budget
totals of main cost items against budget.

Because of the seasonal nature of the work the costs and income do not increase regularly from month to month in a straight line. This coupled with the inevitable lags in the income and costs being accounted for, means that for instance, neither are likely to have reached 50 per cent of the budget by the end of the first six months. Also machinery repair costs may appear very encouraging at the mid-point because the heavy winter overhauls are still to come (see Figure 8.1).

In addition to the detailed monitoring of financial information it is usually possible to have a very up-to-date, but approximate, indication of the financial health of the organization by a weekly monitoring of staff vacancies and overtime working. Any vacancies against a pre-planned staff establishment represent a potential saving and any overtime working an additional cost. Assuming that a premium rate is paid overtime (time and a half) a vacancy for a week is equivalent to:

$$\frac{39 \text{ hours}}{1.5} = 26 \text{ hours of overtime.}$$

Wage costs against budget can then be monitored on a weekly basis as shown in Table 8.3.

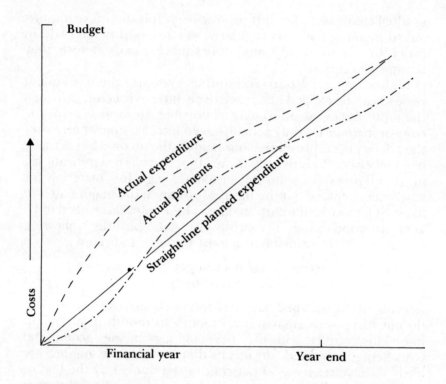

Figure 8.1 *Annual pattern of expenditure and cost recording*

Table 8.3 *Weekly monitor of wage costs*

	Area 1	Area 2	Area 3	Total
				Week No. 14
1. Staff establishment	15	18	16	49
2. Staff in post	14	16	17	47
3. Staff vacancies	1	2	−1	2
4. Overtime equivalent	26	52	−26	56
Overtime				
5. Hours worked	60	42	10	112
6. Credit for the week (4 − 5)	−34	10	−36	−60
7. From previous week	−112	68	−220	−264
8. Carried forward (6 + 7)	−146	78	−256	−324

Total credit/debit in man weeks $\frac{-324}{26}$ = 12.46 debit

Planned man-weeks 14×49 = 686
Percentage variation = 1.8 per cent debit

Chapter 9

A POSTSCRIPT ON SOME FUTURE TRENDS OF LANDSCAPE MANAGEMENT

Most of the landscape in which we live and work has been formed, almost as a byproduct, from the interaction of land use and economic activity. This is clearly obvious in the countryside where the actions of man and the farming methods have slowly established the pattern of the landscape which we enjoy. More recently the balance has been shifting because of changes in agricultural practice and this has increased the demand for the control over rural land use, in particular to conserve or manage the landscape for its attractiveness and for our enjoyment.

In the urban scene the changes from new development or inner city decay are often much more significant and sometimes more despoiling. There is, however, a good deal of 'landscaping' which, in the main, attempts to ameliorate the new development and help it to blend into its surroundings. This landscaping is, almost by its very nature, piecemeal and there are relatively few places where there has been an overall approach to landscape design and development. The new towns are notable exceptions together with urban parks and the historic parklands around large country houses. None the less, of the vast majority of our landscape, there is very little in the way of positive design or management, as distinct from protection from development.

In most large towns, and smaller centres of population, there are significant areas of land set aside for parkland, or for recreation and amenity, and throughout the country many millions of pounds are spent on their annual maintenance and upkeep. Even here, however, there is relatively little in the way of longer-term management and it is the regular maintenance that dominates the landscape which is produced. The fact that the routine care and maintenance is so time-absorbing, and often urgent, means that the organizations responsible for urban landscape are largely maintenance organizations with neither the skills nor the opportunities for analysing the longer-term needs or development of amenity landscapes.

Through lack of positive management their longer-term development tends to happen by chance, largely in response to random external forces such as shortage of money, changing pressures of use and the personal preferences of the maintainers themselves. Inevitably, there are various vested interests in the status quo and so the parks and open spaces tend to lag behind and only respond slowly to changing demands or even to internal decline such as gradual tree loss or other deterioration. Thus it is frequently claimed (often unfairly) that urban parks departments have failed to respond to the recent shift in public taste towards more natural and varied landscapes. Furthermore, it is claimed that the valuable resource that the parks represent is often not used to its full potential.

In areas that have been recently laid out, the landscape architect, through the basic design, will tend to have set the maintenance on a particular course, perhaps for five or so years at least. However, even within that short timespan, the maintenance regimes can begin to alter the course of development and ongoing consultation or understandings between maintainers and designers are relatively rare. Thus, all too often, maintenance is the dominant and only force that shapes the landscape and there is relatively little informed discussion about the maintenance regimes, their costs and eventual results. The regimes are rarely defined in written form, except for the purposes of establishing work routines, staffing levels or bonus incentive scheme payments. Therefore, even that information is largely internal or confidential to the maintainers.

Fortunately the majority of the maintenance organizations are staffed by dedicated and hard-working people and the results are a credit to their skill and professionalism. However, there are strong indications of:

- poor or inappropriate use of resources where maintenance regimes do not appear to match the public aspirations for the sites
- misguided or clumsy attempts to redesign or improve (often in response to cost saving rather than value for money)
- dissatisfaction, lack of interest or even outright abuse of the open spaces by the public who are expected to use them.

None of these things can necessarily be put right but there are two important factors that are likely to change the situation in the future.

1. The increasing awareness of the value of green space in urban centres and therefore the need to manage it more effectively, rather than just maintain it.
2. The implications of the government's compulsory competitive tendering legislation.

The second factor is probably going to be the most significant in that it requires the separation of the maintenance operations, under the contractor role, from that of the overall management, the client role. Thus there is now an obligation to define the maintenance regimes and with it the likelihood that the costs of different regimes and their application to different areas will become much more obvious. In the short term this may lead to even more vigorous cost-cutting exercises, and consequent deterioration, but the clients, or their managers, will have much greater influence over what maintenance and minor improvements are carried out. In essence, the whole planning and budget system could be reversed.

In the traditional model in local authorities, the size of the maintenance organization is set by the annual budget. This budget will normally reflect the staffing needs for the peak of the growing season and these staff, once in post, will use their best endeavours to achieve the results that they consider the most appropriate. Those results will be influenced by the weather, breakdowns and other natural events but, in the off-peak season, a good deal of time will be available for refurbishment, replanting or minor improvements. The volume and scope of these activities will be largely decided by the 'maintainers' who will do as many of them as their time allows. The controlling factor is therefore the ability and aspirations of the maintenance staff.

Under the effect of compulsory competition the client, through its manager, will be obliged to define regimes to be adopted and, by inference at least, the results that are to be achieved. Budgets will therefore be set much less in terms of manpower and machinery and much more in terms of the work to be done and minor improvements or refurbishment projects. This will be a considerable change for many local authorities and, instead of the format shown in Table 8.1, the budget may appear in something like the style of Figure 9.1 with the emphasis on outputs and results rather than inputs.

In order to achieve this approach there will need to be some form of classification of the sites, or parts of sites, according to the levels or costs of the maintenance regimes. In very general terms the more elaborate and formal the maintenance the more expensive it becomes (see Table 1.1) and a simple or basic classification might be:

Type 1   *Ornamental lawns and annual bedding*, e.g. town centre prestige area, formal parks, promenades, etc.

Type 2   *Lawns with shrub borders and/or ground cover*, e.g. building surrounds, school grounds, high quality road verges, etc.
  (a)   To amenity standard – say, up to a weekly mowing cycle with regular clipping and weed control
  (b)   To utility standard – 10–14-day mowing cycle and less frequent clipping, etc.

Type 3   *Extensive grass areas*, e.g. informal open space, large areas of building surrounds or extensive urban road verges.

Maintenance type	Proposed area (hectares)		Budget cost (per unit area)	Total
1. Ornamental lawns and annual bedding	(3.0)	2.5	£60,000	£150,000
2. Lawns with shrubs				
(a) Amenity standard	(63.5)	65	£4000	£260,000
(b) Utility standard	(45)	46	£3000	£138,000
3. Extensive grass areas				
(a) Amenity standard	(140)	126	£600	£75,600
(b) Utility standard	(104)	98	£400	£39,200
4. Housing estate and urban road verges				
(a) Amenity standard	(32)	26	£2000	£52,000
(b) Informal standard	(31)	35	£1200	£42,000
5. Sports grounds	(72)	72	£2500	£180,000
6. Semi-natural grass and woodland	(245)	265	£100	£26,500
Total	(735.5)	735.5		£963,300

( ) denotes figures for the previous year.

Figure 9.1   *Draft annual budget for grounds maintenance 1990–91*

       (a)   To amenity standard – say, up to a weekly mowing cycle.

       (b)   To utility standard – say, a two-weekly mowing cycle.

Type 4   *Housing estate and urban road verges*

       (a)   To amenity standard – say, a two-weekly mowing cycle.

       (b)   To utility standard – say, monthly rotary mowing.

Type 5   *Semi-natural grassland and woodlands*, e.g. hay meadows, wildflower banks, country parks and picnic areas.

This form of classification can be expanded or modified to suit the local requirements but its main function will be to provide a sort of priced 'menu' from which the different alternatives can be extracted.

Once a draft budget has been prepared by selection from these alternatives (see Figures 9.1) there can be a much more informed debate about the levels of maintenance that can be afforded and, if necessary, there can be detailed discussion about the zoning of maintenance regimes on individual sites. The final budget can then be fixed by altering the total areas under different regimes to match the money that is likely to be available. This process will, in turn, help to identify the consequences of any budget cuts or increases, hopefully as an aid to making better value for money decisions.

Even with more informed budget-making processes, landscape as a budget item will still be under considerable pressure from the demands for other local authority services. Many of these services, from mending the roads to providing homes for elderly people, can make strong and justifiable cases for more resources and so landscape managers must learn to 'market' parks and open spaces if they are to be properly financed. The whole process of marketing is a complex one and must be tailored to the local circumstances, but some of the initiatives might include:

- The preparation and publication of 'green' plans, both for local areas and for individual sites
- talks and lectures to amenity societies and the like about the local green space
- the formation of volunteer groups to assist with maintenance or improvement projects, particularly for natural areas and woodland
- guided walks or tours of large parks or footpath systems
- regular newspaper articles or broadcasts about seasonal events and the operation of the maintenance organization.

This sort of marketing is already going on in many places but there is still plenty of scope for more, and for more landscape managers to cope with the new issues that will result from competitive tendering and the separation of management from maintenance. Some developments which have already taken place will help to fill the gaps. In the early 1970s the Landscape Institute, formerly composed entirely of landscape architects, created a new class of membership for professional landscape managers. Although only a small number have been able to satisfy the stringent entry requirements (around 100 in 1988) there are now two new university courses offering degrees in landscape management and the graduates from these will help to swell the numbers coming from courses in related disciplines.

These new managers will have a thorough grounding in the processes of landscape husbandry and amenity horticulture, but they will also have knowledge and skills in, for instance:

- landscape design
- property management and planning law (as it affects open spaces)
- contract preparation and management
- financial and resource management marketing and public relations

Finally, they will also need to have a sound understanding of the business side of landscape management and we hope that this small book will assist them, and all the others who strive to conserve and enhance the landscape around us.

INDEX